HISTORY

OF

CONECUH COUNTY,

ALABAMA.

EMBRACING A DETAILED RECORD OF EVENTS FROM THE EARLIEST PERIOD TO THE PRESENT; BIOGRAPHICAL SKETCHES OF THOSE WHO HAVE BEEN MOST CONSPICUOUS IN THE ANNALS OF THE COUNTY; A COMPLETE LIST OF THE OFFICIALS OF CONECUH, BESIDES MUCH VALUABLE INFORMATION RELATIVE TO THE INTERNAL RESOURCES OF THE COUNTY.

—BY—

Rev. B. F. RILEY,

Pastor of the Opelika Baptist Church.

COLUMBUS, GA.:
Thos. Gilbert, Steam Printer and Book-Binder,
1881.

This volume was reproduced from
an 1881 edition located in the
Evergreen-Conecuh Public Library
Evergreen, AL

Please Direct all Correspondence & Orders to:

Southern Historical Press, Inc.
P.O. Box 1267
Greenville, S.C. 29602-1267

Originally published: Columbus, GA, 1881
Reprinted with new material by,
Southern Historical Press, Inc.
Greenville, S.C., 1994
New Material Copyright 1994 by
Southern Historical Press, Inc.
Greenville, S.C.
All Rights Reserved.
ISBN # 0-89308-692-4
Printed in the United States of America

TO MY MOTHER,

WHOSE ARDENT DESIRE TO TRAIN HER CHILDREN FOR USEFULNESS
FOUND EXPRESSION IN THE MOST UNTIRING DEVOTION TO
THEIR INTEREST, AND TO WHOSE MATERNAL PIETY
AND SACRIFICE THEY ARE MORE INDEBTED
THAN TO ANY THING ELSE,
THIS HUMBLE VOLUME IS AFFECTIONATELY DEDICATED
–BY–
THE AUTHOR.

PREFACE.

ABOUT two years ago, it was suggested that the people of Conecuh take immediate steps toward the preparation of a history of their county. A society was formed bearing the title of "The Conecuh Historical Society;" some interest was manifested, and after several meetings the author was requested to undertake the preparation of the present work. The disadvantages under which he was placed, however, were very great. He lived in a portion of the State remote from Conecuh,—and had the pastoral care of a church, which entailed onerous duties upon him. To secure an accurate record, it became necessary for him to visit the county quite often, and to be in constant correspondence with parties in different portions of Conecuh. But after two years of labor, amid the weighty duties of the pastorate, the work is finished and sent forth upon its mission. The author has striven to present facts in their clearest and simplest form, so that the work would be acceptable to all classes of readers.

If, in some portions, the history be thought too minute in detail, I have to say that this is inseparable from the fact that it is a local history. The work is not as complete in its scope as I would desire to have it. It will be observed that marked details exist with respect to some portions of the county, while they are meagre with regard to others. This is entirely due to the fact that a greater amount of data was furnished me from some quarters than from others.

Special attention has been given to the biographical portion of

TABLE OF CONTENTS.

CHAPTER I.—Page 13.

Introduction—Conecuh in the Earliest Times—Derivation of Its Name—Original Appearance—Abounding Game—Ferocious Beasts—Early Battle Scene, &c.

CHAPTER II.—Page 19.

Early Settlement of Conecuh by the Whites—Conflict at Battle Branch—First Settlement at Bellville—Founding of Hampden Ridge—Alexander Autrey—Other Settlers—Land Claims—Emigration, &c.

CHAPTER III.—Page 22.

Early Privations and Struggles—Unparalleled Difficulties—Scarcity of Shoes—Undaunted Heroism—Meagreness of Blacksmith Facilities—Joshua Betts—A Barefooted Population—Scarcity of Grist Mills—Georgia Currency, &c.

CHAPTER IV.—Page 26.

Indian Hostilities—Troublesome Red Men—Their Depredations—Early Forts—Primitive Means of Defence—Unceasing Vigilance—Retirement of the Indians to the West.

CHAPTER V.—Page 28.

Signs of Advancement—Influx of Population—Industrious Signs Prevailing—The First Store-House in Conecuh—The Court House at Hampden Ridge—Churches—The First Sermon—First School—Conecuh Organized into a County—Public Roads—Anecdote of Hayes and Austill.

CONTENTS.

CHAPTER VI.—Page 33.

A Chapter of Biography—Rev. Alexander Travis—Alexander Autrey—Samuel W. Oliver—Dr. John Watkins—Chesley Crosby—Fielding Straughn.

CHAPTER VII.—Page 43.

Centres of Population—Bellville—Hampden Ridge—Sparta—Brooklyn—Fort Crawford.

CHAPTER VIII.—Page 55.

Centres of Population Continued—Old Town—Fork Sepulga—Burnt Corn—Evergreen.

CBAPTER IX.—Page 66.

An Early Home and Its Surroundings—Now and Then—Mode of Transportation Adopted by the Early Fathers—The Home of the First Year—The Improvement of the Second—House Furniture—The Happiness of Former Times.

CHAPTER X.—Page 70.

Customs and Habits of the Early Pioneer Families—Rude State of Society—Early Amusements—Styles of the Former Times—Horseback Riding—Scenes at Public Gatherings.

CHAPTER XI.—Page 73.

Continued Development—Rapid Advancement—Tides of Population—Gathered Fruits of Toil—Improved Homes—Social Changes—Reverses, &c.

CHAPTER XII.—Page 76.

Transportation and the Inauguration of Postal Routes—Navigation of the Conecuh River—Brooklyn Again—The First Post-Office—Different Mail Lines.

CONTENTS. ix

CHAPTER XIII.—PAGE 79.

A Chapter of Biography—Rev. James King—Rev. Keidar Hawthorne—Joel Lee—Wilson Ashley—Nicholas Stallworth, Sr—John Sampey—William Rabb, Sr—Adam McCreary.

CHAPTER XIV.—PAGE 92.

Conecuh from 1825 to 1835—Current History Resumed—Lull of Apprehension—Fruits of Peace—Tragedy—Rude Customs Still Prevailing—Birth of Political Agitation.

CHAPTER XV.—PAGE 103.

Conecuh from 1835 to 1845—Interesting Epoch—Birth of Political Issues—Excitement Begins—Hot Contests—The Great Indian War—Democrats and Whigs—Hard and Soft Money Issue—Educational Improvements, &c.

CHAPTER XVI.—PAGE 112.

A Chapter of Biography—Hon. J. S. Hunter—Richard Warren—John Greene, Sr—J. R. Hawthorne—J. V. Perryman—Samuel Burnett—H. F. Stearns—John Bell.

CHAPTER XVII.—PAGE 123.

Conecuh from 1845 to 1855—Status of the County at this Period—Acrimonious Politics—Sad Tragedy—Steam Navigation Undertaken Upon the Conecuh River—A Disaster and a Protracted Law Suit—Caterpillars in Conecuh—Mexican War—Sickness in the County.

CHAPTER XVIII.—PAGE 130.

A Chapter of Biography—John Crosby—Rev. Hanson Lee—James M. Bolling—Thomas W. Simpson—Nicholas Stallworth, Jr—A. D. Cary—W. B. Travis.

CONTENTS.

CHAPTER XIX.—Page 145.

Conecuh from 1855 to 1860—Stirring Activity—Progress—Academy at Bellville—Know-Nothingism—County Paper—Railroads and Telegraph—Murder of Allen Page.

CHAPTER XX.—Page 155.

A Chapter of Biography—E. W. Martin—Rev. George Lee—Hezekiah Donald—Churchill Jones—J. W. Ethridge—Sherman G. Forbes—Solomon S. Forbes—M. B. Travis—J. D. Cary.

CHAPTER XXI.—Page 167.

War Record of Conecuh—Intense Excitement—Conecuh Patriotism—Conecuh Guards—Flag Presentation at Sparta Depot—Address by Miss Mathews—Other Companies—Scenes in the Camps at Home—Invasion of the County—Disasters.

CHAPTER XXII.—Page 177.

A Chapter of Biography—James A. Stallworth—William A. Ashley—Rev. W. C. Morrow—J. M. Henderson—Dr. Milton Amos—Dr. William Cunningham.

CHAPTER XXIII.—Page 189.

Dark Sway of Reconstructionism—Social Chaos—Demoralization—Local Troubles—Sovereignty of the Bayonet—The Negro as a Politician—How the New Order of Things Affected Southern Society—Heroism Displayed, &c.

CHAPTER XXIV.—Page 194.

"Peep o' Day"—Darkness Clearing Away—Advancement of Order—Returning Signs of Prosperity—The People Becoming Themselves Again—Glance at Current Events up to the Present.

CHAPTER XXV.—Page 198.

Present Representative Men of Conecuh—Rev. Andrew Jay—Dr. J. L. Shaw—Y. M. Rabb—A. J. Robinson—N. Stallworth—P. D. Bowles—G. R. Farnham.

CONTENTS.

CHAPTER XXVI.—PAGE 214.

Population—Principal Town—Climate—Soil—Stock Raising—Productions—Industrial Resources—Forests—Streams—Numerous Advantages, Social, Educational, Agricultural—Colored Population, &c—Closing Remarks.

APPENDIX.

I.—Constitution of Conecuh Historical Society............Page 223
II.—Roll of Conecuh Guards....................................... " 225

HISTORY OF CONECUH.

INTRODUCTION.

CHAPTER I.

Conecuh in the Earliest Times—Derivation of Its Name—Original Appearance—Abounding Game—Ferocious Beasts—Early Battle Scene, etc.

CONECUH is an Indian name, to which have been given a variety of meanings. But the best translators of the Indian dialect believe its meaning to be "Cane Land," derived from the vast canebrakes which lined its numerous streams, and which covered its extensive tracts of lowlands.

The original word from which the present name is supposed to have been corrupted was "Econneka," which, in the Creek tongue, means "Land of Cane." This is the rendering given by Col. M. H. Cruikshank, of Talladega, to whom the author was referred by Prof. W. S. Wyman, of the University of Alabama. After venturing several conjectures himself, as to the meaning of the word, Prof. Wyman, with genuine good humor, says: "The name Conecuh means *Polecat's Head;* being a compound of *kono*, the Creek word for polecat, and *ekuh*, head." "Then," continues the Professor, "this is my best conjecture, and if it should turn out that I have hit the right meaning, it is to be hoped that the good people of Conecuh will not be unduly distressed at the unsavory name of their county. As the rose by any other name would smell as sweet, so it stands to good reason that the goodly land of Conecuh, swept, as it is, by the resinous airs of its own healthful pine forests, visited by the fragrant breezes of the peninsula of orange flowers, and wooed by a touch of the sultry breath of old Ocean himself, smells sweet in spite of its ugly name." After several conjectures, against all of which he raised some objection, Prof. Wyman urged that the whole matter be submitted to Col. Cruikshank, whose practical knowledge of the Indian dialect enabled him to give the meaning presented on the first page. The county took its name from the stream of the same name which penetrates its eastern portion.

To each of these streams the native tribes gave a significant name, derived from some prevailing characteristic, or from some notable event connected therewith. The statement already made as to the meaning of Conecuh, is further corroborated by the glowing description given by the earliest settlers of the appearance of the face of the country. The virgin forests of Conecuh, as described by the pioneer fathers, must have rivalled in appearance the fairest spots of earth. Before one occupying a prominence there was spread out a scene of panoramic beauty. Vast stretches of land, dipping into occasional basins, ranged visibly in all directions, unbroken by the small undergrowth of shrubbery, which is now a prevailing feature in our forests. The land was radiant with long, waving grass, interspersed with the wild oat and the native pea-vine, and relieved by the monarch pine trees, which stood like so many columns in the great cathedral of nature. Across these smiling landscapes, and through these verdant vales, there roved vast herds of deer and flocks of wild turkeys, together with other game—the evident tokens of a beneficent Providence. Here and there these lands of wild beauty were streaked with clear, flowing streams, the track of whose shining currents could be followed for miles by reason of the native cane, which grew in rank luxuriance along their banks. There was not then, as now, a mixture of tangled shrubbery with the cane along the banks of these streams. The streams themselves abounded in the finest fish, while the lakes and ponds swarmed with countless flocks of wild ducks. From out the thicket jungles there would issue, at night, the hideous growls of wild beasts, the ferocious protests of the native denizen to the encroaching civilization of the white man. Such is the description given of Conecuh when the enterprising settlers first occupied its soil.

EARLY SKIRMISH.

The first item of historic interest is connected with a skirmish on Burnt Corn creek, thirteen miles south of Bellville, which was the commencement of the great Indian War. The settlers along the Tombigbee, having learned that Peter McQueen, with a body of warriors, numbering about 350, had gone to Pensacola for the purpose of obtaining supplies from the British, preparatory to an attack upon the whites, sent Col. James Caller, with a small body of cavalry, to intercept them. Returning from Pensacola, ladened with supplies, the Indians had stopped near the banks of Burnt Corn creek, to rest and cook dinner. Having driven their ponies across the stream to a basin of land, thickly overgrown with tender cane, the dusky warriors lay down in the shade to rest, while the squaws prepared dinner. Coming from the opposite direction the advance guards of Caller's forces found the Indian ponies grazing in the tall cane, and immediately reported the discovery to their commander. With great caution the whites advanced, crossed the stream in single file, and commenced to fire upon the reclining warriors. Snatching up their guns, the Indians ran down under a bluff that overhung the creek. Confident of easy victory, Caller and his men began to plunder the Indian camp and to reap the spoils of success. Meanwhile the brave warriors rallied and returned the fire with vigor, advancing all the while upon the over-confident whites. At the first fire from the savages, the unhitched horses of

Caller's men scampered off in all directions. In much confusion the whites retreated to the top of the hill, and the results would have been disastrous, it is said, had not Capt. Sam Dale covered the retreat with a small body of men. Filled with a new fire of revenge, the Indians, a month later, fell upon Fort Mimms, the horrors of which event were appalling beyond description. When the earliest inhabitants came to Bellville they found the spot where the tribes held their war dance in honor of McQueen's victory over Caller. Thus was spilt upon Conecuh's soil the first blood of that terrible series of sanguinary conflicts, which culminated in the removal of the native tribes to the far West. What a melancholy history is that of the Red Man! The narrative of their unchecked dominion, contrasted with that of their rapid dispersion, is sad beyond measure. The history of their undisputed sway is written upon the rills and rivers of our fair land to-day. As Alabama's once gifted poet, Judge A. B. Meek, has sung:

> "Yes! tho' they all have passed away,—
>   That noble race and brave,
> Though their light canoes have vanished
>   From off the crested wave;
> Though 'mid the forests where they roved,
>   There rings no hunter's shout,—
> Yet their names are on our waters,
>   And we may not wash them out!
> Their memory liveth on our hills,
>   Their baptism on our shore,—
> Our everlasting rivers speak
>   Their dialect of yore!

'Tis heard where Chattahoochee pours
    His yellow tide along;
It sounds on Tallapoosa's shores,
    And Coosa swells the song;
Where lordly Alabama sweeps,
    The symphony remains;
And young Cahawba proudly keeps
    The echo of its strains;
Where Tuscaloosa's waters glide,
    From stream and town 'tis heard,
And dark Tombeckbee's winding tide
    Repeats the olden word;
Afar, where nature brightly wreathed
    Fit Edens for the Free,
Along Tuscumbia's bank 'tis breathed,
    By stately Tennessee;
And south, where from Conecuh's springs,
    Escambia's waters steal,
The ancient melody still rings,--
    From Tensaw and Mobile."

Chapter II.

Early Settlement of Conecuh by the Whites—Conflict at Battle Branch—First Settlement of Bellville—Hampden Ridge—Alexander Autrey—Other Settlers—Land Claims—Emigration.

Subsequent to the defeat sustained by the whites at Burnt Corn creek, under Col. Caller, it seems that a small body of settlers penetrated Conecuh, under the leadership of Capt. Shomo—now of Monroe county— and chastised the Indians at Battle Branch, eight miles south of Bellville. The details of this second conflict are not given. It is said that the marks of the battle are to be seen to-day, in the impressions made in the bark by the flying bullets of the assailants. In the latter part of 1815, the first permanent settlement, by the whites, was made near Bellville. Samuel Buchanan was the first to establish his home within the borders of the county. He located on what is now known as Hawthorne's Mill Creek, about one and a half miles west of Bellville, near the famous Indian trail known, then, as the Old Wolf Trail, which ran from the present site of Claiborne, on the Alabama river, *via* Bellville, to some point on the Chattahoochee. At this period no whites resided nearer this pioneer hero than at Claiborne on the west, or Burnt Corn on the north. But shortly after this, Alexander Autrey removed from the region of Claiborne, and settled upon a small stream west of his late residence, which he called Autrey's creek. Subsequent to this, he removed to the line of hills which overlook Murder creek from the west, where he established himself in a new home, and named it Hampden Ridge.

Shortly after Mr. Autrey's removal to Conecuh, there came from North Carolina three gentlemen whose names were Thomas Mendenhall, Eli Mendenhall, and Reuben Hart. The first of these established himself at the spot now known as the Old Savage Place, on the road running from Bellville to Evergreen. Mr. Hart located very near the present residence of Dr. J. L. Shaw. Early in 1817, the population of Bellville, which then boasted of the name of "The Ponds," from the lakes which existed near, was increased by the emigration of Joshua Hawthorne from Wilkinson county, Georgia, to South Alabama. He pitched his family tent in the virgin forests near the home of the late Henry Stanley, surrounded by no other elements of civilization than those already named.

As each emigrant would take up his abode in this land of teeming beauty, he would cast about him for the most favorable location, and one best suited to the interests of his future residence. In order to fix the title of what was then known as the Emigrant's Claim, the early pioneers would select the tract or district best suited to their tastes, and would proceed to indicate their title to permanent tenure by girding a few trees, with impressions cut in the bark, and by laying somewhere upon land desired, the first four logs of a building. This was a monument of possession, and was sacredly respected by the early settlers. The man who would dare disregard this asserted claim, was branded a rascal outright, and incurred the loss of public confidence and esteem.

Near the period above referred to, another batch of emigrants came to Conecuh from Chester District, South Carolina. They settled near Hampden Ridge. These were Chesley Crosby, Robert Savage, Mabry Thomas, and Alexander Donald—then quite a young man. These were accompanied by Robert Herrin and Jesse T. Odum—the former of whom continued on to Claiborne, where he located and resided many years; while the latter removed to Buena Vista, in Monroe county, where he lived to be quite old. All of these flourished conspicuously in their adopted counties, for many years together.

Chapter III.

Early Privations and Struggles—Unparalleled Difficulties—Scarcity of Tools—Undaunted Heroism—Meagreness of Blacksmith's Facilities—Joshua Betts—A Barefooted Population—Paucity of Grist Mills—Georgia Currency, &c.

Notwithstanding the luxuriant abundance of natural elements, with which the early settlers found themselves surrounded, they were not exempt from the privations then universally incident to pioneer life. Vast forests had to be felled, and the fields to be cultivated, but most scanty was the supply of implements with which the formidable task had to be undertaken; and the few in hand were of the rudest character. A few axes and grubbing hoes, such as the daring emigrants had brought with them from their distant homes, were the only utensils that could be brought into practical requisition.

But with that heroism which had prompted them to penetrate these forest wilds, they energetically addressed themselves to the stupendous task. But at every step, they encountered new difficulties; one overcome, another was introduced. By dint of arduous and tedious toil, the forests were partially cleared away—but where were the implements of agriculture with which the soil was to be tilled? A few shovels, spades and grubbing hoes, of the rudest character, and an occasional scooter plow, were the only implements with which these primitive agriculturists were to raise their virgin crops. The only instrument used by many of the wealthiest farmers, for several years, was a sharply-flattened hickory pole, made somewhat in the shape of a crowbar, with which holes were made in the soil and the seed deposited. An embarrassing difficulty arose from the absence of smithy facilities among the early farmers, and hence many saw but little hope of subsequent relief from their perplexity. This embarrassment, however, was partially overcome in upper Conecuh by the possession of a few blacksmith tools by Joshua Betts. He was reinforced by his brother, Isaac—who had, by the aid of the enterprising settlers in that region, supplied himself with a complete outfit of blacksmith tools, for which he agreed to pay with work done in his shop.

But one of the severest privations to which the pioneer families were subjected was a great scarcity of shoes. Many of the fathers and grandfathers of the influential families now resident in Conecuh, were, from necessity, barefoot laborers. The early soil was tilled, through heat and cold, by barefooted men. The game was chased over the hills by men wearing no shoes. Men and women taught school, and attended church, with feet totally unprotected. And to show that it was not incompatible with primitive dignity, one of the earliest aspirants to Legislative honors—Captain Cumming—actively canvassed the county of Conecuh, on horseback, with his feet clad only in their native nudeness. It is said to have been not an unfrequent occurrence to meet men, on horseback, with their naked feet armed with a pair of rude wooden spurs.

The year 1816 was noted as being one of sore privation to the heroic families who had confronted the perils of these forest wilds, nerved alone by the hope of future reward, which itself was dependent upon their tedious exertion. To appreciate their struggles with formidable difficulties, one has only to be told that during the year 1816 the settlers of Conecuh had to procure their corn from Claiborne, which had to be transported in sacks across the country on horseback—and that, too, amid the constant danger of falling into the hands of roving bands of savages, who prowled like beasts of prey in all directions. This stupendous disadvantage was further enhanced by the utter absence of grist mills; and hence the planters had to have recourse to a rude contrivance of their own manufacture, which was called a "sweep." This consisted of a pestle, fixed into a horizontal pole, which rested upon an upright forked beam, securely fixed into the ground. Beneath this was placed a mortar, which contained the corn. By the perpendicular operation of the pestle, the corn was gradually pounded into a mealy state. This inconvenient usage was at length obviated by the erection, in upper Conecuh, of a grist mill upon the identical spot where Ellis's Mills now stand. This was built by Captain Cumming. Shortly after this, a similar enterprise sprang up on Mill creek, near Bellville. This was erected by Bartly

Walker.* These were the only mills that existed in Conecuh for many years. And such rare enterprises did not fail to become centres of influence for a long time. They were the points of popular resort, whither the fathers of yore would gather, each bringing his ponderous sack of corn on his horse or mule, and accompanied by his trusty rifle. And as the miller would reduce their corn to meal, many would be the feats described, and the adventures recounted, by the hardy fathers of the long ago. Among other hardships encountered by the early inhabitants of Conecuh was that of being forced oftentimes, by stress of necessity, to consume meal made of corn which had molded through age and exposure. And their rapid prosperity becomes to us, more a source of wonder, when, superadded to all these hardships, was that of being compelled to use Georgia currency, which was below *par;* so that even though the injured corn was conveyed from such distances, it cost from four to seven dollars *per* bushel.

But, rising above all these stupendous difficulties, these hardy sons of energy laid the foundations of wealth, and transmitted to the succeeding generation not only the results of their toils, but, besides, the power of a physical and moral courage, whose strength ever rose higher than the confronting barrier, and enabled them to prevail against odds the most formidable. Verily, more than any ever experienced by their offspring, "these were times that tried men's souls."

---

*The mill rocks used here were dug from the earth near Joseph Burt's, where an abundance of similar stones may still be found.

Chapter IV.

Indian Hostilities—Their Depredations—Early Forts, &c.

Contemporaneous with the events already recorded, were occasional outbreaks from the Indians. Relics of the broken tribes were roving in small bands over the wide and wild waste of country. These were the remnants of the tribes defeated and dispersed by General Jackson in the battle of the Horse Shoe. Numerous were the depredations committed by these wild bands. Frequently the carcass of a cow would be found flayed of its skin and with the haunches removed. And woe betide the poor Indian who was found with traces of blood upon his person, or with moccasins of cowskin upon his feet. He was sure to become the recipient of a severe castigation at the hands of the outraged inhabitants. These depredations kept alive the fire of hostility between the white and red races. Stung with the passion of revenge, these bands of hostile Indians would sometimes fall unawares upon an unprotected community, and after speedily wreaking their vengeance, in the work of death upon the defenceless, would again dash off, and stealthily conceal themselves in the jungles of the forest. Bloody scenes were enacted upon the Forks of Sepulga and upon the Conecuh river. In 1818 these bands, having concentrated, felt sufficiently strong to threaten the extermination of the pale faces. The white settlements having learned of their belligerent designs, considerable alarm was produced, and they felt impelled to take immediate steps toward protection. By concert of action in the several settlements, three forts were accordingly erected—one near the house of Alexander Autrey, one at the fountain head of Bellville branch, near the present house of John H. Farnham, and one in the neighborhood of Burnt Corn. The implements of war, like all other works of art, were necessarily scant. Whatever could deal the blow of death, was laid under tribute and conveyed forthwith to these strongholds of protection. The armory of defence consisted of club axes, worn blunt by long usage; knives, old bayonets, gathered from the Indian battle grounds; clubs and old guns. With these implements of protection, the early fathers, together with their families, repaired to these bulwarks of defence. Feeling that "eternal vigilance is the price of liberty," they slept nightly upon their rude arms, and were ready at the slightest alarm, to mete out death to their dusky assailants. As the Indians gradually retired, however, to the Big Warrior Nation, tranquility was restored, and by degrees the people of Conecuh resumed the work which High Destiny had entrusted to their hands—that of lifting the country from its primeval inactivity upon the plane of a progressive prosperity. As the slumbering resources of nature were evoked, energy was stimulated, ingenuity was unfolded, difficulties vanished, the boundless forests disappeared before the axe of advancement, and fields were everywhere abloom with natural increase.

Chapter V.

Signs of Advancement—Industrious Signs Prevailing.

With the restoration of tranquility there naturally came an influx of immigration from the States of South Carolina, Georgia and Tennessee. Civilization now began to find expression in the establishment of social institutions. Commerce, though on a scale quite limited, assumed positive shape. Schools were established. Here and there a church edifice, though quite in keeping with the rough life of the pioneer, was erected, and industry was rearing embryonic monuments all over the face of the country. In 1818 there came to the Bellville settlement a young man whose name was Robert C. Paine. He was half-brother to Mrs. Alexander Travis. Prompted by a spirit of enterprise, he erected, in the Bellville community, the first mercantile establishment ever built on the soil of Conecuh. His store-house is described as having been of exceedingly rude appearance—in apt keeping, however, with the principle of "the eternal fitness of things." It was built of pine poles, unstripped of their bark, and had a dirt floor. The stock in trade of this father merchant was a little coarse sugar, which he sold at fifty cents *per* pound; a little coffee, at one dollar *per* pound; and a few dry goods, suited to the tastes and the necessities of the early families. These goods he hauled in a small ox-cart from Blakely.

While Bellville was thus rapidly asserting her claims to a more advanced civilization, Hampden Ridge (the Autrey settlement) was setting up rival claims. Here the first temple of justice was erected by the aspiring fathers, in the shape of a rude court house. It was built of chestnut logs, was planted full upon a dirt floor, and in regard to furniture, boasted of a rough table, behind which sat the wearer of the ermine in all his primitive dignity. Having but one room, the retiring juries would have to resort for secrecy, and for the formation of their verdicts, under the eye of a vigilant bailiff, to the surrounding forest. Prisoners were conveyed across the country—a distance of thirty-five miles from the prison in Claiborne. During the session of court they had to be guarded beneath the shades of the ancestral oaks, which crown Hampden Ridge. Favorably for the future inhabitants of Conecuh, her earliest settlers were, to a great extent, men of piety. Along with the development of the several bustling communities of the county, there grew up a desire to erect church edifices, to be consecrated to the worship of "the true and living God." About 1817 there removed from Twiggs county, Ga., a Baptist minister, whose name was David Wood. Though blind, he was an earnest, practical, devoted minister of the truth. He preached the first sermon ever delivered in Conecuh county, in a small, rude cabin, which stood on the spot of ground now occupied by the graveyard, near the Bellville Baptist Church. A little later than this, the first school ever instituted in Conecuh was established by John Greene, Sr., near the site of his present home. Among his pupils were the Rev. David Lee, now of Lowndes county; his brother, Ithiel, deceased; Watkins Salter, at one time clerk of the court of Conecuh, and afterward its representative in the Legislature, and still later a representative from Lowndes county; the late Miles Herrington, and Jacob Betts, a prominent merchant at Burnt Corn—then quite a small boy.

CONECUH IS ORGANIZED INTO A COUNTY.

Conecuh did not become a separately organized county until January, 1818. Prior to this time it was embraced within the limits of Monroe county, which then embraced an extensive tract of territory, extending from east to west, from the Chattahoochee to the Alabama. But after the organization of Conecuh into a county, it was bounded on the north by Monroe and Montgomery counties, on the west by Clarke and Mobile, on the east by Georgia, and on the south by Florida—then a Spanish province. Richard Warren became the first representative of the county in the Territorial Legislature, which met then at St. Stephens, in Washington county. Ransom Dean (brother-in-law to Col. J. R. Hawthorne), was the first sheriff, and by virtue of his office, was tax assessor and collector, as well. Joel Lee (the father of Rev. David Lee), was the first justice of the peace appointed in

Conecuh. He was appointed by Gov. William Bibb.

PUBLIC IMPROVEMENTS.

For a long time after the settlement of this portion of Alabama, the inhabitants had to adopt for their highways the beaten trails of the Red Man, which threaded the forests in all directions, and led through the dense cane that skirted the streams, at the only points where it could be penetrated, and where the streams themselves could be forded. To form some estimate of the density of these brakes, which prevailed with uniform impenetrableness along the banks of all streams alike, the present inhabitant of Conecuh has only to be told the following anecdote: On one occasion a gentleman living near Burnt Corn, Captain Hayes, accompanied by his young friend, Jere Austill—afterwards celebrated because of his connection with the famous Canoe Fight—was traveling in lower Conecuh, exploring the fertile lands which lie along Murder creek. Returning after nightfall, they attempted to cross Bellville branch, just where the road now crosses between the village and the house of James Straughn, and became entangled in the glade of cane. After wading through the mud for some time, and finding no relief, in their perplexity they set up a yell of distress, which was promptly answered by Joshua Hawthorne, who hastened to their relief, with several negro men, bearing lighted torches, and extricated them.

In 1822 the first public road that ever penetrated

any portion of the county, was cut by order of the Legislature. It was then about the most important thoroughfare in the State. It ran from Cahaba, *via* Old Turnbull and Bellville, to Pensacola, and was afterwards known as "the Old Stage Road."

Chapter VI.

A Chapter of Biography—Early Heroes and Their Struggles—Frowning Barriers—Unequalled Energy—Moral Giants—How the Basis was Laid—Apostolic Consecration, &c., &c.

REV. ALEXANDER TRAVIS.

The sacred position which Mr. Travis occupied, together with the wholesome work accomplished by him in giving so much moral tone to the character of Conecuh county, demand that he occupy the first place in the biographical sketches of her useful and prominent men. Alexander Travis was born in Edgefield District, South Carolina, on August 23rd, 1790. He was the child of humble, though respectable parents. Having been reared on a farm, he was inured to hard service, and thereby the better fitted for the toilsome duties which awaited him in the latter half of his useful and eventful life. The educational advantages of young Travis were limited—not exceeding an imperfect training in the rudiments of the English. But possessing more than an ordinary stock of native intellectual power, he absorbed much information from divers sources, which gave him a respectable position in society. In appearance, Mr. Travis was tall and dignified, and by the gravity of his bearing commanded universal respect. He was converted in 1809, and baptized into the fellowship of the Addiel Church, in South Carolina. One year later, he was licensed to preach; and in 1813, was ordained to the full work of a Baptist minister. Assuming charge of several churches, he retained his pastorate until his removal to Alabama in 1817. Upon coming to Conecuh, he located near Evergreen, where he resided till his death. Such was the zeal of this consecrated missionary, that he would gather together, as he could, a batch of hearers, from Sunday to Sunday, to preach to them the richness of grace in Christ Jesus. Nor were his efforts vain; for soon he collected a sufficient number of converts together, with those who had previously been members of Baptist churches, to organize a church near his home. Hence he became the founder of the famous Old Beulah Church, situated between Sparta and Brooklyn. This he did in 1818. Nor were his labors restricted to this particular section; for in all directions his energies were exerted in the organization of yet other churches. The sparseness of the population compelled him to take long and trying journeys from week to week. But never did inspired apostle address himself to his work with more alacrity. During the week he was an earnest, active student. His library was a plain English Bible; over this he would assiduously pore, by the aid of blazing pine knots, after his labors in the field. Such was the devotion of this pioneer disciple, that he would leave his home early on Friday morning in order to walk to his appointments, thirty-five miles away. And not unfrequently, in these foot-marches, he would encounter swollen streams; but, nothing daunted, he would strap his saddlebags—which he always carried in his hands—about his neck, boldly plunge in, and swim to the opposite shore. Through his indefatigable exertions, thriving churches were established in different parts of the county, and some in districts quite remote from others. And such was his zeal, his success, his ability as a preacher, and his affable firmness as a pastor, that he remained in charge of several of these churches from the period of their formation to his death. This was true with respect to the Beulah and Bellville churches. Of the former he was pastor thirty-five years; of the latter thirty-two. A large and flourishing interest was established by him in the Higdon settlement, between Burnt Corn and Evergreen. Because of his peculiar parliamentary ability, Mr. Travis was chosen the Moderator of the Bethlehem Association for more than twenty consecutive sessions; and because of his earnest support of education, he was made the first chairman of the Board of Trustees of the Evergreen Academy, for many years together. So evenly balanced were all his powers—mental physical and moral—that he was admirably fitted to the work Providentially assigned him in a rugged, pioneer region.

Elder Travis died in 1852, at his old home, where he had lived full thirty-five years. His death was a public calamity, and was universally lamented. He was emphatically a good man. He was, in many respects, a man of greatness. He was unswerving in his principles, and had the courage of his convictions, which he boldly evinced when occasion required; and yet, in his general deportment, he was as meek as a child. At the pulpit end of Old Beulah Church may be seen to-day by the passer-by, a plain marble shaft, which marks the resting place of this sainted pioneer hero.

ALEXANDER AUTREY

was the second white man to settle upon the soil of Conecuh. His biography, therefore, is inseparably connected with the history of the county from its colonial period. He was born of French and German ancestry, in North Carolina, on January 4th, 1780. On March 5th, 1803, he was married to Parthenia B. Irvin. In 1810 he removed to Georgia, whence he removed to Monroe county, Alabama, shortly after the establishment of peace with Great Britain in 1815. Here he must have remained but a short time, for we find him in the early part of 1816 the founder of Hampden Ridge, on the range of hills west of Murder creek. In stature, Mr. Autrey was tall, rather disposed to stoop, and of lean physique. He practically illustrated in his life what could be achieved by genuine pluck and perseverance. The odds encountered, and the dangers braved by him in coming to Conecuh, only served to stimulate him to more vigorous exertions. He came up from the most straitened circumstances, enduring all the privations of pioneer life, and yet when he died he was one of the wealthiest men in Conecuh.* The controlling traits of his character were an indomitable will and a vigorous energy. Whatever engaged his attention at all, fired him with an ardent enthusiasm. He reared a large family, both of sons and daughters, of whom only one remains—Mrs. C. P. Robinson, of Vermilionville, Louisiana. Mr. Autrey died at his residence on September 22nd, 1857, at the advanced age of seventy-seven years.

SAMUEL WHITE OLIVER.

This distinguished citizen was a native of Virginia, where he was born about 1796. The early portion of his life was spent in Clarke county, Georgia. His literary course was taken at Franklin College, and was fitted for the bar in Litchfield, Connecticut. In 1819 he removed to Conecuh, and located near the new county site at Sparta. He soon associated with himself, in the practice of law, Hon. John S. Hunter. By his ability, Mr. Oliver soon won the confidence of his fellow citizens. In 1822 he was elected first to the Legislature, in which position he was retained by the popular voice of the people for twelve years. In 1834 he was chosen Speaker of the House. Two years later he was elected to the State Senate from Conecuh and Butler, but this position he resigned upon his re-

---

* The writer has heard his mother, whose father Mr. Autrey was, relate what she had often heard her mother state—that she (Mrs. A.) would often hold a lighted torch at night for her husband to deposit his seed in the earth.

moval to Dallas county, in 1837. During this year he was the candidate of the anti-Van Buren party for the office of Governor. But in the contest he was defeated by a majority of 4,000 for Hon. Arthur P. Bagby, of Monroe county. Colonel Oliver died at his residence, on Pine Barren creek, in Dallas county, January 18th, 1838. He was a gentleman of shining qualities, spotless reputation and popular bearing. Had his life been prolonged, he would doubtless have attained great distinction.

DR. JOHN WATKINS

was a distinguished physician, who removed at quite an early period, to Conecuh, where he found himself almost alone, for some time, in his practice. Dr. Watkins was born within a short distance of the scene of General Lee's surrender at Appomattox Court House, Virginia, in 1775. Having received a liberal education, he pursued his medical studies in Philadelphia, whence he was graduated in 1804. He first located at Abbeville Court House, South Carolina, where he practiced in the family of Senator John C. Calhoun. He removed to Alabama in 1813, and located first on the Tombigbee river. Later we find him at Claiborne—the only physician between the Alabama and Chattahoochee rivers. Notwithstanding his decided usefulness in his chosen profession, he was urged to represent Monroe in the Constitutional Convention in 1819, and during the same year was elected to the Senate from the same county.

At quite an early period after the settlement of Conecuh, he removed to that county, where his ability was speedily recognized as a physician. But here again he was destined to share in political honors, for in 1828 he was sent to the Senate from Conecuh and Butler. Several years afterward he was chosen to represent Conecuh in the lower branch of the Legislature. In 1842 his services were again demanded in the realm of politics, and he was chosen Senator from Conecuh and Monroe counties. His devotion to his chosen profession, however, continued unabated, and he was assiduous in the accumulation of scientific works, that he might be the more fully prepared to meet the advancing demands of medicine. Dr. Watkins died at his home, near Burnt Corn, in 1854. He was a man of extraordinary physical powers. In manners he was exceedingly plain, and oftentimes very blunt. The following characteristic anecdote is related of him: He had a patient who had for a long time suffered from extreme nervousness. Dr. Watkins having learned that she had a peculiar fondness for coffee, admonished her to discontinue its use. Having been called to visit her again, he found her with her head resting upon her palms, and leaning over the fire-place, where he spied the coffee pot, poised upon a pedestal of glowing coals. Without ceremony, he knocked it from its position, causing the contents to flow out, and then proceeded to kick it across the room, through the door, and into the yard. But he was universally esteemed for his benevolence and hospitality. His memory will ever be cherished in Conecuh, because of his superior public worth.

CHESLEY CROSBY.

The subject of this sketch was born is Chester District, South Carolina, July 22nd, 1788. Here he grew to manhood, when he removed to Conecuh, which was in 1818. When he came to the county he found a few struggling settlements, there having preceded him but few of the early emigrants. Like all others, he erected a rude house, and commenced his labors in the boundless forests of Conecuh. Along with the growth of prosperity in the county he continued to accumulate wealth, and by dint of energy and economy, had amassed considerable property before his death. Mr. Crosby was the ancestor of a large offspring. Many of these reside in Conecuh, some in adjoining counties, and others in different and distant States. He was a man of many sterling qualities of character. In him the widow and orphan ever found a sympathizing friend. And when convinced of the worth of a public enterprise, no one was more liberal in contributing to its success. A praiseworthy example of his liberality is found in the Baptist church at Bellville, to which he gave in a cash donation $500. In consideration of this marked liberality, a seat, stained with mahogany hue, was prepared for him, and which he occupied in his attendance upon the services of the church. After a long and useful life of seventy-five years, Mr. Crosby died at his home, between Bellville and Sparta, on May 22nd, 1864.

FIELDING STRAUGHN.

Among the earliest inhabitants of Conecuh was Fielding Straughn, who was in very many respects an extraordinary man. He was born in Chatham county, North Carolina, in 1783. In 1817 he came to Conecuh, in the full vigor of manhood, and settled his home where Thomas Robbins at present resides. Such was the hardiness of his physical constitution that he defied all the difficulties encountered by him in this pioneer region. He was a modern Nimrod amid the abundant game that thronged the primitive wilds of Conecuh. It is said to have been a marvel how he could penetrate with bare feet and short-cut trousers, the dense everglades of cane and tangled thickets of briar, as he would chase the flying deer or the retreating bear. Though unlettered, he is said to have been a speaker of marked ability in the religious assemblies, of which he was from time to time a member. In early manhood he had a passionate fondness for pancakes and molasses, and indicated an ambition to become sufficiently wealthy to have them every day, instead of only on Sunday. The object of his gastronomical ambition was finally attained, and finding his desires for other objects increasing with his acquisitions, he declared that every man had a pancakes and molasses point in life which was never reached. Mr. Straughn lived to be quite old, having died in 1867, after reaping his share of the prosperity of the county during "the flush times" of its early history. Because of his calm judgment and extensive practical knowledge, he served the county for a long time as one of her most efficient commissioners. Among other descendants he left two sons—Pinkney and James—the former of whom has been a prominent and useful citizen of Monroe for many years, and the latter of whom has served the county of Conecuh with efficiency, as surveyor, for several successive terms.

Chapter VII.

Centres of Population—Bellville—Hampden Ridge—Sparta—Brooklyn—Fort Crawford.

Reference has already been had to the settlements at Bellville and Hampden Ridge. Between the years of 1817 and 1823 the population of both these points was steadily increased. Several brothers, whose name was Bell, came to Bellville, then called "The Ponds," about 1818 or 1820, and having commenced an enterprising life in this region, they called the village after their own name—Bellville. At Hampden Ridge, the home of Mr. Autrey, as at every advance post in this uncivilized region of country, there was a nucleus formed, around which the elements of growth would accumulate as the stream of immigration would continue to flow. As has already been said, by the permission of Mr. Autrey, and partly by his direction, the first court house of the county had been built on Hampden Ridge during the year 1817. After this there came, in rapid succession, and settled hereabouts, the families of Savage, Charlton, Thompson, John and Duncan McIntyre, Dr. Houghton (who soon after died), Major Bowie, Stringer, Causer, Thomas Hodge and Jesse Baggett, the father of Richard Baggett, of Castleberry, who was the first white child born in the county of Conecuh.

By mutual agreement between the white residents

on Hampden Ridge, and the Indians, whose camps and villages lay beyond Murder creek, this stream was fixed as the boundary. But regardless of the agreement, the savages would now and then cross the creek in predatory bands, and commit depredations upon the white settlers, by stealing their cattle and driving them beyond the stream, and to the headquarters of the tribe at Old Town. So enraged did the whites finally become, that they resolved upon a total suppression of these wrongs. Accordingly they mustered every one who was able to bear arms and moved in a body to Old Town. This, they attacked with considerable spirit, driving the native inhabitants, terror stricken, away. They next proceeded to set fire to their town of huts and wigwams and reduce it to ashes. Flushed with victory, the triumphant whites returned to their homes, no more to be molested by the prowling Red Man. The Indians having disappeared from this region, the whites commenced to remove to the eastern side of Murder creek. Major Richard Warren was the first to venture across the stream and pitch his home in a region so lately filled with peril. He was soon after followed by his son, who located at the point where he died, one mile east of Sparta. During the same year Malachi Warren entered eighty acres of land and built a log cabin on the spot where, afterwards, stood the Rankin House. This cabin was the first building erected upon the site of old Sparta, which, at this period, had not been honored with its classic name. At this point Malachi

Warren opened a place of business that might have been aptly described as a pop-corn grocery. Between the homes of Major Warren and his son, Hinchie, a gentleman, whose name was Spires, located. The place occupied by him was afterwards called the Callahan Place. He was the first to begin the improvement of what has been since known as the Cary Plantation. In 1819, Thomas Watts (uncle to Ex-Governor Watts), removed from Georgia and settled near Malachi Warren's home. During the same year a man named Gauf removed from Tallahassee, Florida, and built below the point where afterwards stood the Rankin House, on the road leading from Sparta to Brooklyn. It was near this spot, too, where the first jail was erected. Mr. Gauf established here the first hotel built in Sparta, and in honor of himself, called it the Gauf House. Like most other structures of this period, this primitive inn was of pine poles and flat upon the ground, and, in the absence of lumber with which to construct shutters for the doors, calico curtains and counterpanes had to be suspended as flaps. About this time there came to this community a Northern physician, whose name was Jonathan Shaw. He engaged board in the Gauf House, and built an office near where the Masonic Hall afterwards stood. It was just subsequent to the events already related, that the court house agitation sprang up between the rival communities of Hampden Ridge and the settlement on the opposite side of the creek. A vigorous effort was being made by the Warrens,

Boykins and Hunters, to transfer the site of the county from Hampden Ridge into their own midst. Alexander Autrey led, in a stout opposition, but the decision of the ballot was against him, and, much to his dissatisfaction, he had to yield. Accordingly, in 1820, a new court house was built, and the village thereupon received the name of Sparta—given to it by Thomas Watts, an attorney, in honor of Sparta, Georgia, from which point he had removed. This second court house is said to have been a slight improvement on the one originally built on Hampden Ridge. It was constructed of pine logs, and was, in size, about 20 by 30 feet, and had two doors. In the absence of a local church edifice, it served the double purpose of temple of justice and house of worship. Another court house—the one consumed by fire in 1868—was erected three years later, by a man named Simmons, from Tallahassee, Florida, and the Masonic Fraternity gave him $500 additional to place the lodge room and attic above. Evidences of improvement began now to become manifest in all directions. The evidences of an ambitious civilization were beginning to show themselves in schools, and in more pretentious forms of business than had hitherto existed. The first school here was undertaken by John McCloud, who taught but a brief period, when he was succeeded by Murdock McPherson. The last named gentleman is said to have been the first Mason buried with the honors of that Fraternity upon the soil of Conecuh. To give marked solemnity to the occasion, a fiddle was brought into requisition, and its solemn tones were evoked in the strain of a funeral march, by a wooden-legged doctor, named Ogden. Anderson and Blackshear, two brothers-in-law, and John and Reuben Dean, built two places of business in this rapidly growing village. And after the removal of the court house, the bar of Conecuh was increased by the location of Samuel W. Oliver, Eldridge S. Greening and John S. Hunter, at Sparta.

BROOKLYN.

Prior to the settlement of Brooklyn proper, quite a community had been formed on Ard's and Bottle creeks. There were in this community, as early as 1818, two stores, owned respectively by McConnell and George Feagin. There was also a school being taught here by Mr. Graham, of Georgia; and a blacksmith shop, owned by John Brantley. No trace of this settlement, which was about six miles northwest of the present location of Brooklyn, remains. The last vestige has been obliterated by plantations. Among the earliest settlers here were Asa and Caleb Johnston, and Aaron Feagin—their father-in-law. They removed from Georgia in 1818. Richard Curry, grandfather to Rev. W. G. Curry, now of Wilcox, was also one of the founders of this community. The first settler of the village of Brooklyn was a man whose name was Cameron. He established a ferry across Sepulga river. Edwin Robinson, from Brooklyn, Connecticut, bought out Mr. Cameron's interest, opened a store, and called the place Brooklyn, for his native village in New England. This occurred in 1820. He was reinforced pretty soon by the location of Dr. Milton Amos, after whom Milton, Florida, was named. Then followed the families of George and Reuben Dean and Benjamin Hart, who had first settled at Bellville. Improvements were rapidly made in the promising village, and thereabouts. A church was erected in 1821, the pastor of which was Elder Alexander Travis; a school was established under Mr. Scruggs; a grist mill contributed to the comfort and convenience of the expanding village; new places of business were opened, and thus Brooklyn became, in 1821, the emporium of trade to Conecuh, and the river, which runs hard by, became the commercial outlet of the entire region of country.

Transportation was begun on the Conecuh and Sepulga rivers in 1821. It is believed that George Stoneham was the owner of the first boat that sailed upon the waters of Conecuh. The inauguration of this movement was but the signal for many similar enterprises; for in rapid succession were boats entered by Messrs. Edwin Robinson, James and John Jones, Starke and Harry Hunter, and Frank Boykin, so that within a few years the river was alive with well-ladened boats, plying between Brooklyn and Pensacola, and when the depth of water would justify it, ascending as high as Montezuma, above Brooklyn. These were keel boats, and would carry from fifty to sixty bales of cotton. In capacity they were from sixty to seventy feet long, and eight to ten wide. They were entered in the Custom House at Pensacola, tonnage paid, and then license obtained for steering into port. But the heroic enterprise of these early inaugurators of navigation on the Conecuh river, deserves more extended mention than a bare passing notice, and hence a detailed account of their reverses and successes is reserved for a subsequent chapter. Fresh additions were constantly being made to the population of Brooklyn, and but a short time after its location, we find the families of Hart, Hodges, Meeks, Manning, Slaughter, Folks, Amos, Turk, Burson, Horton, Lee, Halstead, and several families of the Stoneham relationship. These were, for the most part, men of enterprise, and under their direction the work of advancement went steadily on. Vast tracts of land were cleared in the direction of the river, where were soon some of the best improved plantations in the county. Eleven miles below Brooklyn there was a settlement founded on the river, the first inhabitant of which was Malachi Ethridge, who removed with his family from North Carolina in 1818. This well-to-do colony were not neglectful of the advantages which they had enjoyed in the older States, and hence one of the first considerations was the erection of houses of worship. The first church built in this region was a Methodist house of worship, which enjoyed the pastoral ministrations of Rev. James King—favorably known for many years after, as "Father King." In another portion of the community a Baptist church was erected, under the ministerial auspices of Elders Travis and Ellis.

One of the chief attractions of this thrifty community was a manufacturing establishment, which had been built by Thomas Mendenhall, whose ingenuity at that time was proverbial in all parts of the county. Here he was resorted to, from all directions, as the only manufacturer of chisels, augers, cotton-cards, spinning-wheels and gins. Near the village of Brooklyn is a large cave, known as Turk's Cave. A tradition among the earliest inhabitants has it, that it was a place of resort to the noted highwayman, Joseph T. Hare, and his accomplices. It is said to have been the spot where they stored their treasures, and whence "they sallied forth to rob and murder the traders who plied their vocation between Pensacola and the Indian country."*

FORT CRAWFORD,

now in Escambia county, was one of the points earliest settled in Conecuh. It derived its name from an officer in Jackson's command. Benjamin Jernigan seems to have been the first to pitch his tent in this region. He settled within two and a half miles of where Fort Crawford subsequently stood, and on the west side of Burnt Corn creek, within three-quarters of a mile of the present site of Brewton. This was in the latter part of 1816, or early in 1817. Not more than two or three settlements had been made in the county at that

---

*Brewer's History of Alabama, p. 194.

time. Soon after Mr. Jernigan came here, he was joined by James Thomson, Benjamin Brewton, R. J. Cook, Lofton and Loddy Cotten. At this time the fort was occupied by the Seventh Georgia Regiment. General Jackson was in the habit of visiting the home of Benjamin Jernigan—the father of the venerable William Jernigan, now a resident of Pollard. Mr. Jernigan had removed with his family from Burnt Corn Springs for the purpose of herding cattle for Jackson's army. From the direction of Pensacola, Jackson sent the Jernigan family supplies by the Conecuh river, and many were the annoyances to which the boatmen were subjected by the Indians firing upon them from the thickets along the banks. The army quartered at this point received their supplies from Montgomery Hill, on the Alabama river. They were hauled in wagons across the Escambias to Fort Crawford, where for a time all the citizens of this section went to procure bread. The erection of the fort was commenced in 1817. Prior to this time only temporary earthworks had been thrown up. No Indian settlements were then near; but now and then prowling bands would pass through the country, ostensibly on hunting excursions. They usually encamped about the heads of streams, and built temporary shelters of pine and cypress bark. Sometimes they would linger at such points a week together, and then pass onward. In the winter of 1817, tracts of swamp land were cleared of the trees and rank cane, which were burned in the following spring, and the soil planted in corn. Though unprotected by fences, these cleared spots yielded immense crops. The following year an effort was made to fence with the tall cane, but failed.

Soon after the formation of the settlement, Rev. Radford Cotten, a Methodist clergyman, settled in its midst. He was afterwards joined by Rev. Mr. Shaw, also a Methodist minister. Some time prior to this, services had been from time to time held at the fort by Rev. Thomas Walls, a Baptist minister. These services were held at the request of the officers of the fort. In 1818, a church edifice was built on the west side of the river, about four miles above the fort, at a point called "The Bluff." It is thought to have been erected through the influence of Elder Walls. Near this spot a store-house was also built.

The inhabitants living in the neighborhood of Fort Crawford were devoted to farming and to raising cattle and hogs. As early as 1817 they furnished to the markets of Pensacola vast quantities of pease and pumpkins, which they transported in wagons, and exchanged for such delicacies as coffee. So highly were these farm products valued by the Pensacolians, and so great was the abundance of coffee at that period, that a bushel of peas was readily exchanged for a bushel of coffee. The year 1818 was one of sore trial to this interior settlement. The soil had been most fruitful in its yield, but the resources of the earliest farmers had been subjected to great drain by reason of the constant influx of immigration. Such were the straits to which this region was subjected, that corn was sold for four dollars *per* bushel. During that year the community sent Bartley Colley to New Orleans to purchase supplies of corn, which were shipped to Pensacola. As the Indians persisted in their disturbance of all boats ascending or descending the river, wagons were employed to convey these necessaries across the country. A decided check was put upon these troubles from the Indians, in 1818, by the capture of four hundred warriors, by General Jackson, at Ferry Pass.

In 1818, Mr. Walls, brother to the minister, erected a small grist mill near "The Bluff;" and a few years later, Thomas Mendenhall built a saw mill above Fort Crawford. Very little of the lumber sawn here was sold to the citizens, and Mr. Mendenhall, aided by a man whose name was Rolly Roebuck, transported his lumber on rafts to Pensacola. Prior to the erection of this mill, the "whip saw" had been used to some extent in the community. The lumber with which were built the houses of the officers of Fort Crawford, was sawn with the "whip saw." Other timbers were cut and rafted down the river to Pensacola. The readiness with which man adapts himself to surrounding circumstances is strikingly illustrated by the unique plan adopted here by the residents for conveying the products of their diminutive farms to a favorable market. These fresh bottom lands were abundant in their yield of pumpkins. In order to ship these to Pensacola, a huge cypress was scooped out, somewhat in the shape of a mammoth batteau, and of sufficient capacity to hold three hundred pumpkins. With a cargo like this these heroic farmers would speed away down the river, and Pensacola reached, their golden fruit was readily sold—realizing for each pumpkin twenty-five or fifty cents—and rejoicing, they would return.

Game abounded here, as elsewhere in Conecuh. But, strange enough, the community about Fort Crawford was destitute of dogs. To obviate this disadvantage, the officers of the fort, having become very intimate with Willie Jernigan, then a boy of sixteen, engaged him to "play dog" for them in routing the deer from their hiding places at the bushy heads of the streams. With many a bark and yelp, he would plunge into the thick coverts, and the affrighted deer would scamper out in all directions, only to be greeted by the leaden bullets of the officers from their stands.

When, in 1819, it was determined to erect a court house on the east side of Murder creek, Benjamin Jernigan, R. J. Cook, Allen and Alexander McCaskill, Mabry Thomas, and several others, were chosen by this community to select a site for its erection. As has already been stated, the point fixed upon was Sparta.

Chapter VIII.

Centres of Population (Continued)—Old Town—Fork Sepulga—
  Burnt Corn—Evergreen.

OLD TOWN.

The settlement of this point by the whites was made about 1820 or 1822. Within this period there were residing here Richard Curry, who had settled first near Brooklyn; Joel Brown, Matthew Ray, William Rabb, Sr., Levi T. Mobley, Capt. Wilson Ashley, Adam McCreary, John Scoggin, and —— Cravey. This point seems to have been a favorite one with the original resident tribes. It appears to have been a chosen halting place on the great trail that ran from some prominent point on the Chattahoochee to Pensacola. It is supposed, from its original size and apparent importance, to have been the headquarters of some of the tribes. Here was an extensive community, with all the evidences of having been for a long period occupied. The huts, the patches of ground, the extensive play-grounds and the order in which they were kept, the marks on the trees, the neighboring streams, and the cool, perennial spring, which bursts from amid the hills near the old camp-ground —all these would indicate that it was a point of unusual importance with the native inhabitants. But the chief object of attraction, to the early white settlers, was a memorable tree, which still stands as a source of wonder to the passer-by, and is known by the familiar name of the "Old Flag Tree." Its name is derived from the banner-like shape of its branches at the top. For six or eight feet the trunk is utterly bare of branches, when they assume the shape of a flag by growing in a single direction. There was a tradition among the early white settlers to the effect that this towering tree was a signal to the Indian traders passing from the Chattahoochee to Pensacola, as it was to all the bands prowling through the country. The first white settlers who occupied this point were an enterprising colony. Improvements were begun at once. With characteristic energy, William Rabb, Sr., erected a grist and saw mill on Old Town creek. Joel Brown soon followed with the construction of a water-gin, the first built in this portion of the county; while Thomas Lord proceeded to open a small stock of goods—the chief commodity of which was cheap whiskey! But four or five miles beyond Mr. Lord's store, William Rabb, Sr., began merchandising upon a more respectable scale, having ample supplies of groceries and dry goods to meet the demands of the growing community. Scoggins' Meeting House was the first place of public worship in this section. And the devotion of the people was manifested by a ready disposition to walk to church, on occasions of worship, the distance of seven or eight miles. Others, more favored, would come on horseback, or in carts and wagons. The families of William

Rabb, Sr., and Adam McCreary were classed *elite*, because the former owned an old time gig, and the latter an ordinary Jersey wagon. At this period, postal facilities in the county were exceedingly meagre. The nearest post-office to this community was at Sparta—thirteen miles away. An occasional newspaper would stray into the community of Old Town, and it was sacredly preserved, by the fortunate possessor, until the first general gathering of the people, when, by common consent, some one was appointed to read the marvelous harbinger aloud—and this was done to the infinite delight of the eager crowd circling round.

FORK SEPULGA.

The stream, between which and Duck creek this settlement was formed, derived its name from a compound Indian term, *Sucka Pulga*—which means Hog's Creek. A tradition, derived from the Indians, is to the following effect: The Indians lost a large herd of swine from drowning in the stream where Sowell's Bridge now spans the creek. The native tribes were accustomed to drive hogs, fattened on the luxuriant mast in the oak and hickory swamps of Lowndes and Montgomery counties, to Pensacola. A drove of these hogs having been drowned at the above mentioned point, the name *Sucka* (hog) and *Pulga* (creek) was given it; and for convenience, the Anglo-Saxons have corrupted the name into *Sepulga*.

The inhabitant who first settled in this region is said to have been Richard Sermons, who came here in

1818. He was soon followed by Ely Stroud, John Houston, Harrison Harris and Billy Thompson. Later still, we find the homes of Drury Dean, Jesse Cone, Thomas Pigot, Joshua Calloway (a Methodist minister), and Jacob Page—the father of Allen Page (who was murdered near this region), and grandfather to the late P. D. Page, Esq., of Texas, and Haskew Page, now of Sparta. Among the earliest residents here, too, were Abraham Baggett, the grandfather of Rev. Dr. Hawthorne, and William Wetherington. As in all other new settlements, the first improvements here were those born of the absolute necessities of the inhabitants. And almost invariably, if not strictly so, a grist mill was the first public enterprise. Thomas Pigot was the first to meet the public demand in this particular. He constructed a mill upon one of the branches of Duck creek. He subsequently added to his original enterprise a cotton gin. A mercantile establishment had its existence under the auspices of Messrs. Gallagher & Farley. They commenced business, with a substantial stock of staple goods, about 1823. They were succeeded by T. M. Riley, Sr., now of Pineville, Monroe county, who purchased their entire stock in 1826. This point of trade was the same as that which has been long known, by the later inhabitants of the county, as Jackson's Store—the name having been derived from that of two brothers, Wiley and Andrew Jackson, who succeeded Mr. Riley as merchants at this point.

At an early day a church, each, of the Methodist

and Baptist denominations, was built within the circuit of this community. The first Methodist minister who served in this region was Rev. Joshua Calloway; the first Baptist pastor's name was Rev. Keidar Hawthorne—the father of Rev. J. Boardman Hawthorne, D. D. The settlers in this part of the county were the subjects of much annoyance from the Seminoles for some time after they located in this inviting region. These depredations were summarily checked, however, in 1818, by General Pushmattahoy— familiarly known as "General Push"—coming to the relief of the settlers with a band of ninety warriors. General Pushmattahoy was a native Choctaw, and friendly to the whites. Placing himself at the head of his chosen warriors, and a few white men, he attacked the Seminoles, who retreated toward the Conecuh river, but were overtaken and captured somewhere in eastern Conecuh, and brought back, *via* Midway, to Fork Sepulga. These Seminoles were sent forward to the Indian Reservation, west of the Mississippi.

BURNT CORN.

At quite an early period in the history of Conecuh, James Grace removed from Jackson county, Georgia, and commenced the improvement of a home very near the present village of Burnt Corn. He was the first settler in Conecuh, upon its northern border. Two years later he was followed by the families of Joshua Betts, Thomas P. Jones, George Kyser, John Greene,

Sr., Samuel Salter, Richard Warren, Joel Lee, Garrett Longmire and Harry Waldrom. These settled, within a circuit of a few miles, during the years 1816 and 1818. There was an unsteadiness in the population for several years together—a constant shifting of location on the part of the settlers. This was due to a disposition to test the lands in all directions before a permanent settlement was made. Nor did this restless spirit cease until the lands were permanently bought at Cahaba, in 1819. With advancing time the population of Burnt Corn continued steadily to increase. Among the most enterprising and public spirited of the emigrants was Captain Hayes. He was a man of wealth and influence. He built the first frame house erected in Conecuh, which still stands, a monument to his taste and enterprise, and is now occupied by William Betts. Near the residence of Captain Hayes a store-house was erected by Mr. Walker in 1822. He is said to have had a substantial stock of dry goods and groceries.

Near Burnt Corn, Captain Hayes purchased an extensive tract of land, of eleven hundred acres—all of which he enclosed in a single fence, and would continue to clear and improve as it was needed. In 1822 he is said to have erected the first gin-house built in Conecuh. He also established a good mill near Burnt Corn.

As much, perhaps, as any other this community was harassed by the Indians. The inhabitants shared in the consternation produced in all parts of the county; and in Monroe, in 1818. So intense did the excitement become, that some of the residents of this portion of the county joined others leaving Monroe, and fled into Clarke county, where they remained until the restoration of peace. In order to provide against the attacks of the Indians, Major Richard Warren, an old chivalric South Carolinian, erected a rude stockade, into which he invited the terror stricken inhabitants to take refuge every night. This kind offer many accepted, and during the intervening day they would resume their accustomed pursuits. But this state of feverish excitement and alarm so paralyzed the energies of the inhabitants that they were unable to cultivate their little fields. Every distant sound was construed into a danger signal, and so much time was thereby lost, that the result was an almost total failure of the crop. John Greene, Sr., bravely refused to enter the stockade, but remained at his home and continued to cultivate his crop, and the consequence was he reaped a full harvest in autumn. With the restoration of tranquility, the fugitive emigrants returned from beyond the Alabama river, and resumed the improvement of their homes. There came together with them into Conecuh, many who had fled from other portions of the country. Among these I may mention David Jay, the father of Rev. Andrew Jay, who, sharing in the stampede, had gone from the region of Pine Orchard, in Monroe county, to Bassett's creek, in Clarke. Together with Nicholas Stallworth, whose overseer he subsequently became, he returned from Clarke county in 1820, and located about four miles southeast of Evergreen, on what is still called the Stallworth Plantation. After spending about three years here, Mr. Jay removed to the community of Old Town.

DERIVATION OF BURNT CORN.

Many inquiries have been raised, and conjectures made, relative to the origin of the peculiar name—*Burnt Corn*. Rev. David Lee, whose father was a prominent citizen in this section during its earliest settlement, states that near the large spring, which bursts from beneath the hill below the village, there was the residence of a friendly Indian, whose name was Jim Curnells, and that this Indian gave the following as the real origin of Burnt Corn: Two Indians were returning from Pensacola and stopped at this famous spring to camp. During their stay here, one became sick and was unable to prosecute his journey. His companion grew impatient and resolved to leave him to his fate, not, however, without first having supplied him with a quantity of corn, which he poured in a heap on the dry leaves near the suffering man. Recovering from his sickness, the Indian found himself without a sack into which he could put his corn, and left it heaped upon the dry leaves, which caught from the camp fire, and the corn was partially burned. Travelers, stopping here to camp, found the pile of charred corn, and called the spring *Burnt Corn Spring*. As trivial as the occurrence was, the foregoing statement deserves great credence as coming from Jim Curnells. During the war of 1812, this friendly Indian was quite serviceable to the American army, and frequently served as courier, carrying important messages from one point to another. In consideration of his invaluable services, the Federal Government donated him 640 acres of land, including Burnt Corn Spring.

EVERGREEN,

now the thriftiest village, perhaps, in South Alabama, received its first installment of emigrants in 1819 and 1820, though the village itself did not find a name until years afterward. When James Cosey, George Andrews and the Messrs. Cluff, first reached this section, the present site of Evergreen was a tangled wild-wood, revelling in dense thickets of briar and cane, with the jungles infested by the native deer, wolf, bear and wildcat. The tiny streams, that still wind their way through different portions of the village, were then strongly barricaded on either side, with impenetrable brakes of cane. And such was the nature of the soil, which skirted the streams, that it was peril to man or beast to tread upon it. Upon the arrival of the emigrants already mentioned, Mr. Cosey and the Messrs. Cluff located within the limits of the present village, while Mr. Andrews pitched his tent upon the hill beyond the small branch, west of Evergreen. Mr. Cosey was an old Revolutionary soldier, and bore the mark of a severe wound in his bosom. Additions were soon made to this diminutive population, for during the years already named there came several other families, among which were those of William Jones, Sr., and George Foote. Of the entire population, Messrs. Andrews and Foote had removed from South Carolina, the others from Georgia. Living contiguous to the vast swamps which border Murder creek, this settlement was peculiarly exposed to the inroads of the bear, the wildcat, the deer and turkey. The bear and wildcat preying upon the pigs, and the less offensive deer and turkey riotously assailing the ripening grain of autumn. Benjamin Hart erected, at an early day, a good mill, which is now known as the E. C. Smith mill. While subjecting the natural barriers, and wrestling with the grave disadvantages, whose name was legion, these early fathers were not forgetful of the intellectual improvement of their children. About 1820 or 1821, George Andrews opened a small school, about three-quarters of a mile east of the present location of the court house. This gentleman was the father of H. M. Andrews, of Bellville, James W. Andrews, of Allenton, Wilcox county, and of the late George R. Andrews, of Monroeville. In its early history, Evergreen gave but little promise of becoming the important point which it is to-day. Located considerably in the interior, it was regarded as being remote from most of the points first settled. For more than an entire decade it was the most insignificant of all the centres of population in the county. But the gradual settlement of the adjoining regions, the rapid improvement of the fertile lands, in the midst of which it is fortunately located, the early educational advantages which it afforded, the importance given it by the Mobile & Montgomery Railway, and the location of the court house at this point, have helped to render Evergreen conspicuous alike as a mart of trade, an educational centre, and a village unequalled in the State for the moral tone of its population.

Chapter IX.

An Early Home and Its Surroundings—Mode of Transportation Adopted by the Early Fathers.

The marvelous changes which have been wrought in our habits and customs, in private and public life, within little more than half a century, deserve some notice at our hands. The prosperity which has been enjoyed almost uninterruptedly by the people of Conecuh is, in large measure, due to the assiduity of the early founders of the society of the county. The fatigue endured, the self-abnegation, the perils braved, and the obstructions overcome, deserve favorable notice in this work. Never did an ancestry deserve more that their heroism be sacredly enshrined in the memory of a posterity. The homes of comfort, nestled amid natural delights; the extensive and fertile districts of land; the numberless facilities of an advanced civilization; the wealth gathered through years of toil—all this has been secured to the posterity of a heroic ancestry. Starting from their remote homes in the Carolinas or Georgia, and even from Virginia, these early heroes and heroines were aware of the vast distance that lay between them and their future places of residence in the far South. A wagon or two, drawn by horses, or mules, or oxen, were the sole means of transportation enjoyed by an early emigrant for the removal of his family and chattels.

Stopping at night, the family would rest beneath the sheltering folds of a huge tent. This served as a residence, even after the arrival of the family at their final abiding place, until a more substantial home could be established. With very many families, the method of transportation was inferior, even, to that above referred to. Some regarded themselves peculiarly fortunate in being able to secure a huge waterproof hogshead, into which were tightly packed the effects of the family, after that a long rod had been inserted lengthwise. There was sufficient projection of the rod at either end to enable it to serve as a sort of axle. To these points was fitted a pair of rude shafts, to which was hitched an ox. The movement of the animal gave revolution to the great receptacle, and over long leagues, reaching across the broad areas of States, the faithful ox would draw the unique car, even to the final destination of his master. This reached, the first care was to clear off as large a plot of ground as possible, preparatory to the erection of a temporary dwelling. This was constructed after the following model: Four corner posts were fixed upright in the ground, near the tops of which were fastened two small poles, facing each other, and extending around the four sides of the square. Between these opposite pieces was left sufficient space to insert small saplings, which were driven securely into the ground. Over the top of this clumsy abode were thrown the curtains of the tent, which had served the family in its migration, besides the skins of animals. No care was given, the first year, to a floor for the temporary home. The heroic settler had to content himself with pounding into firmness the surface of the ground within this rude enclosure. Even the erection of such a rude domicile as this made a heavy draught upon his time. That which most concerned every one was the production of the first crop. But the second year gave the earnest settler more leisure for the erection of a comfortable house. This was built of hewn logs, which rested upon sills, which in turn were supported by four corner blocks of wood. The roofing was of boards, or rather slabs, riven from split timber. To hold them in position, weight poles were used, which were held at equal distances apart by means of knee pieces. The flooring was constructed of logs cloven into two parts, with the flat surface turned upward. Within this enclosure might have been seen, at the end opposite the family fire-place, a rude bedstead, which was erected in a corner of the room. A single fork, driven through the flooring, served as the support of two beams, which formed the side and foot pieces of this uncomely couch. Meeting in the fork, these pieces of timber were inserted, respectively, into the end and side of the dwelling,—and thus the frame of the bed was erected. Upon this rough contrivance were placed the pieces of timber having the flattest surface. Oftentimes another frame of similar make would be seen in the opposite corner. Some of the family would occupy these beds, while others would lie upon pallets spread on the hard floor.

If emergency demanded the existence of more apartments than one, this was speedily effected by means of curtains and counterpanes, so swung in conjunction with the walls of the corner, as to form a separate room. Cooking was usually done without doors, over a blazing fire, unless the harshness of the weather forbade it. From the centre of the chimney within the dwelling there were suspended the antique "pot-hooks and hangers." One could rarely enter a home of the olden time without finding a huge gobbler, or a leg of venison, swung on either side of the fire-place. During the day the father and sons would till the soil, while the good mother and sisters would serve the cooking, and wake the forest echoes with the live hum of the spinning-wheel, which was usually blended with the spirited songs of these industrious women. The early night was spent around the hearth, made bright and cheerful by blazing pine-knots; and if any member of the circle could read with satisfaction, he was usually assigned this work, while the others joined in the customary labor of carding, spinning, or sewing. And seated thus upon their rough blocks of wood or rude stools, there was enjoyed much of that domestic happiness which has been lost to generations later, even amid the glitter of an advanced civilization.

Chapter X.

Customs and Habits of the Early Pioneer Families—Rude State of Society—Early Amusements.

Much in regard to the simplicity of the manners of the early pioneer families will be gathered from what has already been said. The constraints and conventionalities which increase with a developing state of society, found no exception here. Society was composed of men who were bound together by strong ties. A feeling of mutual dependence produced a feeling of mutual esteem. This they sought occasion to evince as they would ofttimes come together in the chase, at the "log-rolling," or at church. Here they freely mingled together, and were controlled as gentlemen by the dictates of natural judgment and good sense. The wives, sisters and daughters would meet most frequently at quiltings,—occasions which served the double purpose of profit and pastime. The occasion of preaching was hailed with delight. Everybody attended, and every one joined with a genuine heartiness in the sacred worship. No laws of dame Fashion were then transgressed by attending church barefooted, so long as this was regarded a necessity. So highly prized was a pair of shoes during these early times, that the fortunate possessor would guard against tramping in them the entire distance to church, by carefully wrapping them up, and carrying them under his arm, until near the place of worship, when he would proceed to wipe the dust from his feet, insert them into his shoes, and stroll onward to church. Or else, men and women, who had each a pair of old and new shoes, would wear the older within a short distance of the place of worship, and then proceed to displace them with the newer ones, while the others were concealed until their return.

Means of conveyance were exceedingly scant. The father and husband would sometimes be seen approaching, on a public occasion, with his wife behind him, and his children disposed upon the back of a faithful horse, as they could find sufficient space. No violence was done the rules of social etiquette when a gallant youth would offer a blushing damsel a seat behind him on his horse. Where social gatherings were less frequent than now, these people of artless customs were loth to separate. Drawn together from distances far apart, and meeting but seldom, they would quietly listen to quite a long discourse on occasions of sacred service; and when the exercises were over, they would mingle informally together, and render the occasions doubly profitable and attractive to themselves by a free interchange of thought on spiritual experience. After an hour spent thus pleasantly together, a cordial invitation was extended by those living nearest the place of worship, to go with them to their homes and dine. Here was dispensed the freest hospitality, and in the simplest manner, much to the enjoyment both of the entertainer and the entertained.

The favorite amusements of the least spiritual of the male population were shooting matches, foot races, and boxing and wrestling contests. The rude athletic sports, though always begun good-humoredly, were not unfrequently converted into occasions of "rough and tumble" fights. But the primitive "code of honor" forbade the use of sticks, pistols, or knives. Every contestant would have to depend solely upon his natural resources, should he so far forget himself as to be betrayed into a spirit of belligerency.

CHAPTER XI.

Continued Development—Rapid Advancement—Tides of Population—Gathered Fruits of Toil—Improved Homes—Social Changes—Reverses, &c.

Never was any section more rapidly populated, perhaps, than was Alabama, during the decade following 1819. The flood-gates of immigration seemed hoisted, and great swollen currents of human masses poured in from Virginia, the Carolinas, Tennessee and Georgia. During the most favorable seasons for journeying, the ferries along the Chattahoochee were crowded with immigrant trains. Not unfrequently a family would be checked in its progress, for several days, because of the jam and pressure upon the ferries. Their destinations reached, these heroes and heroines would begin at once to lay the rude basis of a house in the way already described. All the while, the older settlements were making rapid strides in advancement. The sound of progress was heard on every hand. Such was the yield of every returning harvest, that the zeal of the immigrant was constantly stimulated. For as soon as the axe levelled "the giant progeny of the crowded trees," and the warmth of the sun reached the soil, upon which had been accumulating, for ages, stratum on stratum of vegetable mould, the productiveness was immense. Homes, too, were improved. The rude hut of the pioneer settler was displaced by cozy and attractive residences. Skilled educators were sought, and schools, of as high grade as possible, were established. The toils of the spiritual laborer were at length rewarded by the erection of neat houses of worship, filled with devout audiences. The increase of population, the advancement in prosperity, and the growing ambition everywhere evinced by the inhabitants of the county to surround themselves with the comforts and conveniences of life, gave new spirit to merchants of enterprise, and hence centres of business were being rapidly formed. Indeed, all branches of industry were being constantly improved. Each revolving year set the stamp of advancement upon the face of the country. This had the double effect of stimulating the energies of the inhabitants and of holding forth a tempting inducement to the residents of the older States to cast their fortunes, too, amid the primitive settlements of Alabama. But the luxuriant prosperity of Conecuh county was destined to sustain a severe check. Either heedless or ignorant of the fact, that behind the screen of the dense everglades that lined the streams and swamps, there lurked a poisonous malaria, the energetic farmer swept down all alike. The fearful consequence was that this invisible foe to health and happiness, crept forth from its impure retreat, and smote with sickness all that came within the reach of its infectious power. Nature surrounds our stagnant swamps with a luxuriant growth of vines and hanging moss, to protect the inhabitants from the pestiferous exhalations; and when this barrier is swept away, there comes forth disease, shaking us with chills and filling our bodies with the venomous seeds of sickness. This calamitous mistake the early inhabitants of Conecuh made. Finding the lands to increase in fertility as they gradually approached the swamps, they at length invaded the marshes themselves, and even increased the intensity of the malarial power by ditching, thus exposing to the sun the unearthed vegetable matter. As a consequence, there was a wide-spread prevalence of bilious and malarial fevers, and many fell victims to their fatal ravages. A perfect panic was produced, especially in lower Conecuh. Several young physicians died. And such was the consternation among the settlements that many left and returned to their homes in the older States, or else removed to counties more northward. The oldest inhabitants of the county to-day refer to 1824 as a year of fatal sickness.

Chapter XII.

Transportation and the Inauguration of Postal Routes—Navigation of the Conecuh River—Brooklyn—The First Post-Office—The Different Mail Lines Established.

Products seek a market as the rivers do the sea. The productive yield from the virgin soil of Conecuh naturally sought an outlet, especially when as inviting a market as was Pensacola in 1821, was within such easy reach. As has already been intimated, the navigation of the Conecuh and Sepulga rivers was undertaken in 1821. Mr. George Stoneham, having inaugurated the movement, was speedily followed by a host of others, prominent among whom were Edwin Robinson, James and John Jones, Starke and Harry Hunter, and Frank Boykin. These rude crafts were called keel-boats, and would carry a cargo of fifty or sixty bales of cotton. In capacity they were from sixty to seventy feet long, and from eight to ten feet wide. By common consent the following was fixed upon as a scale of prices for the transportation of freight: A bale of cotton weighing 300 pounds, $1.25; weighing 450 or 500 pounds, $1.50; corn in the shuck, 18¾ cents *per* bushel; flour, *per* barrel, $1.25; sugar, *per* barrel, $1.25; salt and coffee, $1.25 *per* sack; molasses and whiskey, $1.50 *per* barrel; iron, 50 cents *per* hundred weight. Freight generally averaged about 37½ cents *per* hundred weight. Farmers, furnishing their own blankets and provisions, were cordially invited to accompany these freight-laden crafts, so long as their capacity would warrant. No charges were made for the transportation of such self-sustaining passengers. These primitive boats were steered by means of a beam being fixed at each, the bow and stern, and two at either side. Ascending the stream, a far different method had to be adopted. An instrument, familiarly known among the early boatmen as the "hook and jam," was indispensable to moving these clumsy barges up stream. This instrument was a long smooth pole, of considerable strength, pointed with an iron spike, and with a hook curving its beak but a few inches from the point. The point was used for giving propulsion to the boat by being pressed against the nearest trees, or the banks of the stream. The hook was serviceable in being hitched in the overhanging boughs, which also aided in the propulsion of the craft. Such was the rapid increase of population, and the consequent increase of demand for transportation, that at one time there were seventeen boats, of various sizes, on the Conecuh river. These varied in capacity from five to two hundred bales of cotton. Competition has been ofttimes quoted as being "the life of trade;" but the rule has not been without such exceptions as to prove that it may be the *death* of trade. Such was the ambition, among these early navigators, to control the transportation on the river, that freight was reduced to the minimum price of fifty cents *per* bale from Brooklyn to Pensacola, and up freight correspondingly low. The importance of Conecuh river as a commercial outlet may be estimated when the reader is told that, even as early as 1823, there were annually shipped from Brooklyn three thousand bales of cotton. The passage to and from Pensacola was usually made with comparative ease; and yet more or less peril was apprehended when the river had been cleared, and the barges floated out into the open sea. Gull's Point, in Pensacola Bay, was an object of peculiar terror to these early boatmen. If this could be passed without encountering adverse winds, it became a subject of common congratulation among these primitive propellers of the oar.

The first mail route that penetrated any portion of Conecuh was along the Old Federal Road—which, for a considerable distance, divides the counties of Conecuh and Monroe. The first office was established at Burnt Corn. A branch route was subsequently established between this point and Sparta. This postal service was originally performed on horseback, and at a later period in stages along the principal routes. With the rapid growth of population, post-offices were eventually established at all the principal points in the county.

Chapter XIII.

A Chapter of Biography—Rev. James King—Rev. Keidar Hawthorne, and Others.

REV. JAMES KING.

The writer was fortunate enough to find an autobiographical sketch of the life of this sainted preacher, in the hands of his daughter, Mrs. John Sampey. She very kindly surrendered it for publication, and it is herewith submitted:

December 10, 1856.

This day the Conference met at Tuskegee, being the day that closed my 74th year; and being present with this large body of ministers, numbering about two hundred, it caused my mind to run back over the past scenes of my ministerial life, with deep and very solemn reflections. In contrasting the past with the present, I have thought proper to write down a brief sketch of my ministerial life, with a few incidents connected with my history, which are as follows:

In 1800, I attached myself to the Methodist Church. The society which I joined was composed of six women and one free black man—he being the classleader. In 1802, I married and took upon myself the responsibilities of a family. In 1803, I was appointed the leader of the class which I had joined. In 1805, I was licensed an exhorter. In 1806, I was licensed a local preacher. By this time the society had increased to the number of seventy. In 1816, I was ordained deacon, in Wilmington, by Bishop McKendree; that being the first ordination ever conferred in that place. Up to this date my family had increased to nine in number, beside myself and wife. I remained in North Carolina until 1818, making twelve years. During this time my ministerial labors were confined to six counties, to wit: Bladen, Brunswick, Hanover, Cumberland, Roberson, and Columbus, with some occasional visits to Horee District, South Carolina. In view of the charge upon my hands looking up to me for support, it will be easy to perceive that my labors were extended beyond the ordinary grounds of a local minister; and for all this service and labor I had no claim upon the church, nor did I receive one cent for my labors. On the 21st of April, 1819, I removed with my family to Alabama. I arrived at Alabama Town, where I met with some of my North Carolina friends, who prevailed upon me to stop there for the year. My ministerial labors during that year were as follows: One Sabbath at Alabama Town—the next at Philadelphia (now Montgomery.) I was the first licensed preacher that ever preached in that place. This was one of the years of great trial and privation to me, there being no regularly organized society, and I heard but one sermon preached during the time. In the winter of 1819, I removed to Conecuh river. There being but few settlements at that time, my labors were somewhat curtailed; but

I had two appointments—one above and the other below the Florida line. In the winter of 1820, I moved higher up, into the Burnt Corn settlements, in the bounds of what was then called the Conecuh Circuit, belonging to the Mississippi Conference. This circuit, at that time, covered nearly all that part of Conecuh county that was then settled, and a considerable part of Monroe county. Here, a field was opened wide enough for my labors. In 1822, I was ordained Elder, at the Bellville Church, by Bishop George and others. This circumstance brought upon me a greater amount of labor. The Mississippi Conference, being weak, could not afford an ordained preacher for all the circuits. For four or five years there was no regularly ordained preacher sent to Conecuh Circuit, and consequently it devolved upon me to attend all the societies around the circuit to administer the ordinances of the church. Up to 1830, I continued to travel and labor in that section of the county. In 1830, I lost my wife, which was a severe trial to me. Having three daughters with me, I proposed to them to make their homes with three of their sisters, who were then married, and that I would join the Itinerancy. To this proposition they were opposed, preferring to remain at their own home. Consequently I consented to remain with them, and to do the best for them I could. In 1832, I married the second time. At this time one of my daughters had married, and the other two had gone to live with their sisters.

HISTORY OF CONECUH.

In the spring of 1834, myself and wife removed to Middle Tennessee, where we remained until the close of 1835. My labors during that time were confined to three counties, to wit: Weatherford, Bedford and Williamson, and I attended five campmeetings during my stay there. In the winter of 1835, I removed to Wilcox county, Alabama, and settled a short time afterwards. At the request of Bishop Andrew, I consented to confine my preaching for one year to the colored people, for the purpose of arranging a mission. For this service I received one hundred dollars from the Missionary Society; all is told that I ever received for my ministerial labors. From that time up to 1850, I continued my labors in Wilcox and adjoining counties. In 1851, I lost my second wife. This circumstance changed my situation, and placed me under the necessity of breaking up for good. Since that time, being relieved of the cares of a family, I have devoted my time, as far as circumstances and feebleness would permit, in extending my labors to a wider field.

I have been three rounds with the Presiding Elders down on the west coast of Florida; one round on the Lowndesboro' District, and as far east in this as Dale and Pike counties; from thence west across the State as far as Sumter, and the southern portions of Mississippi. I have visited the above named State three times, in its northwestern counties; and I have also made three visits to my native State—North Carolina. And in all my travels I have preached as often as circumstances would allow. And, in conclusion, what is in the future, is impossible for me to foresee; but of one thing I am assured, that it is my settled purpose to devote the remainder of my life to the service of God and his church. Whereunto I subscribe my name.

[Signed] JAMES KING.

It will be seen from the above article that my labors have been scattered over seven States, to wit: North Carolina, South Carolina, Georgia, Alabama, Florida, Mississippi and Tennessee.

[Signed] J. KING.

Mr. King died in Wilcox county, on January 12th, 1870, at the advanced age of eighty-seven years.

REV. KEIDAR HAWTHORNE

was a native of North Carolina. He removed from Robinson county, in that State, to Conecuh county, Alabama, in 1817. Six months after his arrival in Alabama, he enlisted in the United States Army under General Jackson, and continued with him to the close of the Indian War, in Florida. After his return to Conecuh, he settled near Bellville, where he was married to Martha Baggett, in 1825. It was just subsequent to this time that both Mr. and Mrs. Hawthorne became the subjects of renewing grace, and were baptized by Elder Travis. About two years afterward, Mr. Hawthorne was licensed to preach the gospel, and after serving as a licentiate a short time, he was ordained by Elders Travis and Ellis. A door of opportunity opened to him in the Forks Sepulga, and he forthwith directed his attention here as an inviting field for the exercise of his ministerial powers. A flourishing interest was established by him in this growing section.

Leaving this region, he removed to Mount Moriah, in Wilcox county. He founded the Baptist church at that place, known as the Fellowship Church. Living at a period when there was quite a scarcity of ministers, his services were broadly demanded, and hence he became thoroughly identified with every denominational interest that sprang up in the counties of Wilcox, Monroe and Conecuh. He aided in the constitution of most of the churches in these counties. Perhaps the most remarkable period of his career was the service which he rendered in Eastern and Middle Florida, as a missionary. His labors here were peculiarly blessed. In 1856 Mr. Hawthorne removed to Mobile and established a book-store, at the same time serving with efficiency the Stone Street African Church—one of the largest in the South. Mr. Hawthorne reared quite a useful family, several of whom attained to marked distinction. One of his sons, Gen. Alexander Travis Hawthorne, was a chivalrous officer under General Price, in the Trans-Mississippi Department, during the late war. Another of his sons, Rev. Dr. J. Boardman Hawthorne, has a national reputation as a pulpit orator.

Like many others, Elder Hawthorne suffered the tota   of his estate by the war, but he was tenderly cared for by his children to the close of a long and useful life. He died in Greenville, Alabama, in 1877. Some estimate of his wonderful usefulness may be had when the fact is related that, during the years of his active ministry, he baptized more than 4,500 believers. His ministry extended over more than fifty years.

JOEL LEE, ESQ.

Among the first who set foot upon Conecuh's soil was the subject of this sketch. Joel Lee was born in Johnston county, North Carolina, January 4th, 1773. Forty-four years after this date he removed to Conecuh county, choosing for his home a spot about three miles from Burnt Corn. Here his usefulness was speedily recognized, and he became one of the most prominent citizens in this section. When Alabama became a State, and Conecuh was made a county, Mr. Lee became her first justice of the peace. He was appointed by Gov. William Bibb—Alabama's first Governor. In 1821 he became a member of the Old Bethany Baptist Church, and was baptized by William Jones, Sr. In his church relations his usefulness was as conspicuous as it was in the walks of public life. For many years he served his church efficiently as clerk and deacon. Under his wholesome influence there grew up a large and useful family. Three of his sons were eminent ministers of the gospel. One of them still remains a venerable monument of piety, and a sage counsellor in Israel. I refer to Rev. David Lee of Mount Willing, Lowndes county. Joel Lee died at his home, near Burnt Corn, on October 23rd, 1863.

CAPT. WILSON ASHLEY

was among the most useful of Conecuh's sons. He was a native of Barnwell District, South Carolina. His entrance into public life was quite early. When in 1814 the struggle with Great Britain was pending, Mr. Ashley, then a youth of eighteen, joined a volunteer rifle company, of which he became the first lieutenant. He afterwards became the captain of this company, and subsequently the captain of a cavalry company. He removed to Alabama in 1820, and located within a few hundred yards of where he spent the remainder of his life. In his new home his attention was directed altogether to husbandry. The results of his energy and skillful management soon showed themselves in a growing fortune. In 1832 he was called from his favorite pursuit and was made the sheriff of Conecuh county. Three years later he was chosen, without opposition, to represent his county in the General Assembly of the State. At the expiration of his term of service he peremptorily declined further honors at the hands of the people of the county, and returned to the quietude of his rural home. Here he remained until 1861, when the stirring scenes of that period drew him again from his seclusion. In the election of President and Vice-President, of what was designed to be the permanent government of the Confederacy, Capt. Wilson Ashley was honored by the people of his State with a position on the electoral ticket of Alabama. This closed his career with public life. Mr. Ashley was noted for his suavity of manner, his penetrating discrimination, and his clear judgment. Once convinced of the righteousness of the cause in which he was enlisted, and his zeal knew no bounds. He had all the elements necessary for a political leader of the people. In his home, he was proverbially hospitable. In his social relations, he was cheerful and generous. Full of years, well spent, and endeared to a host of friends and relatives, he closed his eyes in death in the 74th year of his age.

NICHOLAS STALLWORTH, SR.,

was one of the original settlers of Conecuh. Born in Edgefield District, South Carolina, on April 25th, 1777, he removed to Clarke county, Alabama, where he remained but one year. The hostilities of the Indians having subsided, in 1818 he, together with several others, removed to the east side of the Alabama river. He located his home four miles southeast of Evergreen, on what is now known as the Evergreen and Brooklyn public road, where he continued to reside until his death in 1836. Mr. Stallworth was constitutionally fitted to brave the perils of a pioneer country. With robust frame, determined will and unlimited energy, combined with business tact and shrewdness, he rapidly accumulated a handsome fortune, and became one of the wealthiest men in the county. He was the ancestor of quite a number of descendants, some of whom attained marked distinction.

JOHN SAMPEY, SR.

Among the best and most useful of Conecuh's earliest inhabitants was John Sampey, Sr. His birthplace was Belfast, Ireland, where he first beheld the light on April 20th, 1801. In September, 1824, he sailed for America, and reached New York some time during the following month. His tastes having led him to the new regions of rapidly growing America, he came to the inviting State of Alabama, then just looming into prominence, and settled upon the soil of Conecuh. His attention was directed at once to stock raising, and he soon populated the grass grown districts of southern Conecuh with herds of stock cattle. The energy with which he addressed himself to his chosen vocation soon became proverbial. The ancestors of Mr. Sampey (Sampier) were French. They were driven by religious persecution from France during the 16th century, and sought refuge in Ireland. The subject of this sketch was originally a devout member of the Church of England, in which he was reared; but upon removing to Conecuh he became a member of the Methodist Church, in which he spent a devoted life. Mr. Sampey was remarkably quiet and unostentatious. His career was one of evenflowing uniformity. He was scrupulously exact in all his transactions. Was careful never to allow a note to mature without being promptly met. His eyes were closed in death at his old home, near Bellville, on July 8th, 1877.

WILLIAM RABB, SR.

Among those who have contributed to dignify the early annals of Conecuh county by an unobtrusive, yet virtuous life, may be classed the subject of the present memoir. William Rabb, Sr., was born in Fairfield District, South Carolina, on January 10th, 1775. His father was born in Ireland. Mr. Rabb's mental training was defective, because of the meagreness of educational advantages during his early life. During his youthful days he realized the fearful responsibilities of the present life, as connected with the life to come, and without delay gave his heart to God. At this time he joined a Presbyterian church, but in 1835 his church relations were changed by his union with the Old Beulah Church. In 1804 he was married in Edgefield District, South Carolina, to Miss Sarah McDonald, of Scotch parentage. With his family, he removed, in 1819, to Conecuh, and settled what was subsequently known as Rabbville, or Rabb's Store, five miles east of Evergreen. This was one of the first voting points established in the county. Here Mr. Rabb proceeded to merchandising and farming. His goods were hauled across the country, from Pensacola, by his own teams. Like most of the pioneer fathers, who had been attracted from their homes in distant States, Mr. Rabb was active and energetic, and shared largely in the fruits yielded by the virgin soil of Conecuh. He was noted for his liberality, and gave largely to the relief of suffering humanity. His days upon earth closed on September 20th, 1859. His family physician remarked that it was the first natural death he had ever witnessed. There was no disease, no expression of pain, but a placid sleep, ebbing out in death. He sank

> ——"As sinks the morning star,
> Which goes not down behind the darkened west,
> Nor hides obscured amid the tempests of the sky,
> But melts away in the light of heaven."

ADAM M'CREARY

was the ancestor of the extensive relationship of that name still to be found in Conecuh and adjoining counties, and indeed in different States. He was born in Barnwell District, South Carolina, about 1772. He removed to Conecuh county in 1818. The struggles and perils of his youthful life thoroughly inured him to hardship, and fitted him for what he had to encounter in a wild region, such as was Conecuh when he removed thither. While he was quite a boy he endured some of the horrors of the Revolution. His father's home was located in that region which was so sorely infested by the Tories. Fearful lest her son might have to pay the penalty of his father's patriotism—for he was in the ranks of the regular army— the anxious mother would send her son, in company with a negro boy, to sleep, at night, in the woods.

Upon his removal to Conecuh Mr. McCreary selected, as the place of his future residence, the thrifty little community of Old Town. He was the first to improve the present home of Dr. Taliaferro. In disposition, Mr. McCreary was quiet and passive. His Christian deportment was almost without exception. Such was his veneration for the Scriptures that he drew therefrom the names of all his children. His views were exceedingly hyper-Calvinistic, and quite frequently, in the midst of calamity, he would seek relief in the assurance "that it was foreordained, and therefore right." On one occasion, a negro boy, belonging to him, made an inroad upon the smoke house of his Antinomian master, and when arraigned for the deed, took refuge in the favorite doctrine of his owner, saying, "Well, Massa, you see all dis was 'ranged fore hand. It was all fore'dained dat I should take dat meat!" Stung by the evident sarcasm, and exasperated by the complacent impudence of the thief, the master bound toward him and caught him in the collar, saying, "And it is foreordained that I give you a thorough thrashing, and I'll do it!" After a long and useful life, spent in Conecuh, he died at his home, in 1844, in the 72nd year of his age.

Chapter XIV.

Conecuh from 1825 to 1835—Current History Resumed—The Lull of Apprehension Among the Inhabitants—The Fruits of Peace—Tragedy—Rude Customs Still Prevailing—The Birth of Political Agitation, &c.

The current history of Conecuh was broken at the point where reference was had to the wide-spread sickness among the inhabitants of the county in 1824. Sufficient attention having been bestowed upon the events which gathered around that period—to the personages, too, who flourished at that time, giving so much character to the dawning history of the county—we resume at this point the continuation of the current record of events. The disease of the previous year had spent its force, and the citizens, having become acclimated, or else having removed with their families to higher and healthier locations, resumed with unabated vigor the work of development. The period, about which I now write, was one of very great tranquility. The circles of population were being enlarged in all directions, more extensive tracts of land were being annually cleared, and the prosperity of the county was settling down upon a solid basis. The oldest and most improved plantations were now exceedingly productive, and their owners were growing rich. As yet no political venom, with its attendant demoralization, had been injected into the social mass. Quietly every man attended to his own affairs at home, or else, acting in concert with his neighbors, would engage in the erection of churches and school houses. The martial spirit imbibed from their contests with the Indians and British, was still retained by the inhabitants, and places for general drilling were appointed in different parts of the county. This gathering gave occasion for having a gala-day, and its recurrence was ever hailed with delight. To these different points the male population would repair, *en masse*, each man carrying with him his fowling-piece; and after evoking all the delights that could be drawn from a straggling, dusty and irregular drill, they would gather about the place of trade, lounge in the shade, exchange rude jokes, recount perilous adventures, wrestle and box, and not unfrequently become contestants in a tumbling hand-to-hand fray. But, however much puffed the cheek may have been, or however much bunged the eye, or enlarged the nose, every one usually repaired, at the close of day, to his own home bearing no malice toward his neighbor. These pugilistic rencounters, let it be said, were usually confined to the "lewd fellows of the baser sort," each of whom coveted the distinction of "bully." Refinement by degrees predominated and these barbarous practices were gradually abandoned.

Returning to the thought of the growth of development, let me say that but little attention was bestowed upon any occupation except that of farming. Indeed, "farmer" was quite a comprehensive term.

Many of the farmers combined merchandising with agriculture. A farmer was very frequently both a merchant and carpenter; for there was not sufficient trade to engage the entire time of one man, and hence the store was made secondary to the farm. And again, in such a rude state of society, the only architectural knowledge required was that which enabled one to erect a rude cabin with cloven logs. Hence, farming was the chief vocation. For the most part, the inhabitants who first settled Conecuh had removed from wheat-producing regions; and this cereal they undertook to raise in Conecuh, and for the first few years, were remarkably successful. But, either because of the decline of the fertility of the soil, or because it was found to be so much easier and more profitable to produce corn and cotton, its production was gradually abandoned. Another consideration which led, perhaps, to its abandonment was that the harvesting of wheat conflicted sadly with the attention which was necessary to be given the cultivation of corn and cotton. And another consideration, still, was that the wheat was smitten with rust, which was discovered to increase with each advancing year.

As in all new regions of country, where Nature is munificent in her gifts, these are sadly abused ofttimes by the earliest recipients, so in this favored region the pioneer fathers manifested, in some respects, a most reckless prodigality in regard to their fertile lands. This, however, was, in part, due to their ignorance of the utility to which many elements could be applied, and partly to a lack of sagacity. For many years after the production of cotton had begun, the seed were regarded a nuisance after that they had been removed by ginning from the fabric. The idea of employing them as a fertilizer, to arrest the decay of lands, was not suggested to the thrifty fathers. Hence they were hauled away and thrown into abandoned heaps.

The wisdom of arresting the washing of lands, seems never to have been suggested to the primitive farmer. Of course, the best lands were the first to be improved, as they were quite frequently the first to be abandoned as having become useless through wear. As a consequence, many of the lands which were originally the best to be found in the county, were speedily surrendered to the sedge-grass and the needle-leaved pine, and are to-day regarded as barren wastes. With a more compact population—which our county is destined, at no distant day, to have—these wasted fields will be reclaimed from desolation, and again be made to "blossom as the rose."

A few years after the first settlement of the county another branch of business sprang into existence—that of stock raising. The luxuriant pasture lands that composed the southern portion of the county, reaching even down to the coast, were covered with vast herds of cattle. The largest among the herds was that of David Tate, a half-breed, whose cattle swarmed over the grassy districts stretching between the Big and Little Escambias. Higher north, a herd of four thousand was owned by John Sampey. This branch of trade has ever been one of profit, and is destined, in the history of the county, to become one of the most lucrative of her industries.

In 1825, a Land Office was established at Sparta, with Dr. Jonathan G. Shaw, of Massachusetts, as Receiver. He was appointed by President John Quincy Adams. Considerable excitement prevailed among the people of the county at this period in consequence of the spirit of speculation that existed in certain quarters. Keen-eyed speculators were industrious in seeking out the best lands in the county, the claims of whose occupants were not secure, and in putting an enormous estimate upon their value in order to realize, in their sale, considerable profit. This produced widespread dissatisfaction and demoralization. To avoid being dislodged from the place improved by himself, Rev. Alexander Travis purchased his land of these Shylocks at the exorbitant sum of $37.50 *per* acre. But so grave an imposition upon a quiet, industrious community, such as Conecuh had become, could not go unrebuked and unchecked. The grievances of the indignant masses reached the ears of Congress, and the Relief Bill was passed, causing the late sale to be cancelled and the lands to be re-purchased. Mr. Travis now secured his land, under this bill, for $1.25 *per* acre. And what was true of him was equally true of others. This brought a protracted period of tranquility and prosperity to the people of Conecuh.

The successful navigation of the Conecuh river, and the enormous revenue which the owners of the boats on that stream were realizing, led to an effort to navigate Murder creek.* Accordingly the services of Colonel Bowie were secured to clear the stream, and prepare it for the passage of boats. Several ineffectual efforts, however, convinced the inaugurators of the enterprise that it was by no means feasible, and the project was abandoned at once. While this attempt was a bootless one, it only served to show that the spirit of enterprise was abroad in the land. By every means the inhabitants sought to utilize the facilities with which nature had so prodigally supplied their adopted home. Continued advancement served to stimulate the energies of the thrifty population, and each recurring year witnessed a marked change in all portions of the rapidly growing county. Lands were being improved by a more thorough system of drainage, and the rude contrivances of the early colonists were being eventually displaced by substantial evidences of advancement.

In 1827, a tragedy occurred at Ellis's Mills that shocked the entire county. Captain Cumming, who had, for some years, been conspicuous in different ways in the county, was killed by a man whose name was Fuller. Naturally impulsive, and of a domineering disposition, Cumming attacked Fuller with a storm of abuse, to which no resistance was offered. Stung by this cool indifference, Cumming went away and

---

*This beautiful stream derived its name, according to Colonel Pickett, in his History of Alabama, vol. II., page 82, from a bloody tragedy enacted upon its banks in 1788.

carefully loaded his gun for the express purpose of killing Fuller. Fired with passion still, he returned to the place where Fuller was quietly at work hewing a log, and walking within a few feet of him, he levelled his gun at his breast, pulled trigger—and it missed fire. At this juncture Fuller sprang forward, with his broad-axe, and drove it into Cumming's skull. He quietly surrendered himself to the proper authorities, but was duly acquitted.

While the material interests of the county were being steadily advanced, regard was had to the moral enlightenment and spiritual improvement of the people. The ministry of this period were ardently devoted to the promulgation of the truths of the gospel, and their laborious exertions bore fruit in the form of thriving spiritual interests, which were being planted within convenient reach of the growing population. The consecration of Revs. Alexander Travis, Keidar Hawthorne, John Ellis, and William Jones, Sr., of the Baptist denomination; and of Revs. James King, Joshua Calloway, John A. Cotten, and Lewis Pipkin, of the Methodist Church, is sacredly enshrined in the memories of the oldest residents of the county. The recollections of these sainted pioneer preachers will never be embalmed in "the flower-crowned annals of song," but better, they will be transmitted with pathetic interest to the future generations of the county.

An event took place in the region of the Burnt Corn settlement, in 1828, that deserves special notice in the History of Conecuh, as indicating both the assiduity of Elder Travis and the generosity of John Greene, Sr. Ministerial laborers being but few in the county, and Mr. Travis being anxious to have the gospel preached to as many as possible every Sabbath, conceived the plan of centralizing the interests in different portions of the county. In upper Conecuh there had been established, by himself and his co-laborers, several points where preaching was had as often as a minister could, in turn, visit them. He determined upon a combination of these several interests, and appointed a committee to select a site for the erection of a house of worship sufficiently commodious to accommodate these congregations when formed into a single church. Finding the committee somewhat embarrassed by their inability to fix upon an eligible spot, Mr. Greene very generously offered them a tract of land, northwest of his dwelling, as a spot suited to the erection of a church edifice. The lot thus donated by himself was covered with a grove of beautiful oaks, from the midst of which flowed, perennially, the waters of a bold spring. The terms of the donation were, that the tenure of possession was to be commensurate with the occupation of the place as a point of worship. The generous offer was gratefully accepted, and the church became famous as a place of worship in this portion of the county. In after years the church was removed to Puryearville, in Monroe county, and became the Old Bethany Church.

Among the enterprises which were inaugurated in the county during the following year (1828) was one that sprang into existence as if by magic. This was a point of business of unusual interest, that was established just below Bellville, between the Fergurson Place and the residence of Thomas Simpson, Sr. This enterprise was established under the auspices of a young man, from Mobile, whose name was Hosefield. His place of business was contiguous to an old field, whose broad, level acres presented an inducement to the county militia-men as an admirable place for "mustering." So important did this point become, as a place of thriving trade,—and so notorious was it for rowdyism,—that the inhabitants named it "Little New York." After a few years' existence, it disappeared with the suddenness with which it originally began. A slightly cleared place is the only relic now remaining of one of the most notorious points that existed in the county of Conecuh.

The political questions of the period, which had already commenced their turbulent sway in the older States, had not as yet reached Alabama. The Carolinian element, which entered so largely into the early population of Conecuh, shared somewhat in the exciting Nullification movement, which stirred so deeply the public sentiment of South Carolina, in 1832. But it gave no shape or color to the politics of this region, as did no other question at this time. It was reserved for later years to witness all the bitterness and rancor that are born of heated political discussion. At this period of the history of the county, voters were not controlled in their preferences by the complexion worn by any political organization, but altogether by the reputation of the candidate. The contests in the realm of politics were based upon no pronounced issues. Sometimes there was but one candidate before the people—at other times there was quite a host. The most formidable opponent was he whose integrity was most unquestioned and unsuspicioned, and whose personal influence was such as to sway the masses. Long before this period—perhaps as early as 1820 or 1822—election precincts had been established at the homes of William Brewer, William Blackshear, and David Hendricks, at Cumming's Mill; also at Zuber's Store, George Constantine's, Brooklyn, James Caldwell's, Rabb's Store, James Grace's, and John Bell's.

About 1833, a startling event occurred in the region of Fort Crawford. A woman, whose name was Mrs. Nancy Taylor, had gone to the home of a neighboring woman and had given her a severe drubbing. The violent assault evoked judicial interference, and Deputy Sheriff Dollyhide was sent by Sheriff Wilson Ashley to arrest the turbulent woman. When Mr. Dollyhide reached her house, she positively told him that she would not be taken. Walking coolly up to her side, he laid his hand upon her shoulder, and said: "Madam, you are my prisoner!" She instantly snatched from her bosom a sharp dagger, and drove it to the hilt into the heart of Deputy Dollyhide, and he fell dead at her feet. Dressing herself in the costume of a male, and in company with a kinsman, whose name was Fed Walker, she fled to Texas, leaving behind her husband. He remained in Conecuh for another year, when he, too, emigrated to Texas, and rejoined his fugitive wife.

The following is a list of the members of the General Assembly from the county up to the period of 1835:

SENATORS.

1819—John Herbert.
1821—John W. Devereux.
1825—William Jones.
1828—John Watkins.
1830—William Hemphill.
1833—William Hemphill.

REPRESENTATIVES.

1819—William Lee, Thomas Watts.
1820—Samuel Cook, Thomas Armstrong.
1821—Eldridge S. Greening, John E. Graham.
1822—Samuel W. Oliver, John S. Hunter, ——— Taylor.
1823—Samuel W. Oliver, John Fields, James Salter.
1824—Samuel W. Oliver, Nathan Cook, John Greene.
1825—Samuel W. Oliver, Eldridge S. Greening.
1826—Samuel W. Oliver, Eldridge S. Greening.
1827—Samuel W. Oliver, Eldridge S. Greening.
1828—Joseph P. Clough, James Salter.
1829—John Greene, Henry E. Curtis.
1830—Joseph P. Clough, Samuel Dubose.
1831—Samuel W. Oliver, John Watkins.
1832—Samuel W. Oliver, Julian S. Devereux.
1833—Samuel W. Oliver, Watkins Salter.
1834—Samuel W. Oliver.
1835—Wilson Ashley.

CHAPTER XV.

Conecuh from 1835 to 1845—Interesting Epoch—Birth of Political Issues—The Excitement Begins—Hot Contests—The Great Indian War—Democrats and Whigs—Hard and Soft Money—Educational Improvements, &c.

We now enter upon the history of one of the most interesting decades in the annals of the county. The political questions which had grown out of the existing state of the government, and which had crystallized into positive shape in the older States, had been transferred to the extreme South, and gradually shaped themselves into principles upon which the voters of Conecuh were divided. Just enough interest had been awakened by the exciting Nullification movement in South Carolina, to inspire a desire to read, and hence the leading political papers of the country were being eagerly subscribed for. This spirit received encouragement, too, from a combination of favorable circumstances, in which the people of the county were now placed at this advanced stage of their history. These circumstances were—the growth of population, which drew the masses more frequently together; the increased postal facilities of the county; the more intelligent generation that was coming upon the stage of action; and the greater leisure afforded by the advanced prosperity of most of the citizens of Conecuh. Notwithstanding the intense excitement produced by the

Nullification struggle, it was destined to be followed, within a few years, by a discussion, the excitement of which, if it did not equal the intensity of the former, it exceeded it in general interest. This was the discussion of the great Bank question. A subject so important, and of such popular interest, touched all classes of persons alike. In the midst of the sternness displayed by President Jackson, which unpoised the financial system of the whole country, producing a serious crash in 1837, Thomas H. Benton, Senator from Missouri, urged the adoption of a gold and silver currency, as the true remedy for the embarrassments of the times. This financial question drew the line of demarcation very broadly and clearly between the two existing dominant parties—the Whigs and Democrats—the former of whom opposed the measure suggested and advocated with so much power by Mr. Benton, while the latter, with heartiness, adopted them. The two parties became very pronounced in the enunciation of their respective views. This period witnessed the first political contest, upon clearly defined party issues, that was ever had in the county of Conecuh. True, divergent views had been held by her people prior to this time, and minor differences had been expressed in a feeble way; but now excitement ran high, and the respective parties rallied and drilled their forces for a hot contest at the ballot-box. They selected their candidates for the Legislature, the Democratic nominee being J. Richard Hawthorne, and that of the Whig Party being Jephtha V. Perryman. Because of his enthusiastic advocacy of hard money principles, Mr. Hawthorne won from his opponents the sobriquet of "The Benton Mint Drop Boy." After a thorough and exciting canvass of the county, the election resulted in the choice of Mr. Perryman by just seven votes. This election, for a time, put a quietus upon the county, the Whigs being exhilarant over their victory, while the Democrats were encouraged to renew the contest, by the fact that they came so near of success. At this period of the county's history, public attention was diverted to a more serious question than that which agitated the people at their homes—this was the outbreak of hostilities on the part of the Indians. The policy of the government of removing them from their old abodes, which was instituted in 1832, had met with resistance almost everywhere. Both along the Chattahoochee and in Florida, there were hostile demonstrations. A call was made for troops, and in response, Captain Bell, of Bellville, raised a company and went to Georgia. Of those who were members of that company, the names of none can be secured, except those of Absalom Autrey, Pinkney Straughn, and Madison Crosby.

Whatever of interest there was in the history of the county for several successive years following 1836, it gathers around the fierce contests which were waged in the political arena from year to year. For a number of elections together, the Whigs were the successful contestants. 1839 is famous in the annals of the county as being a year of remarkable prosperity. The oldest citizens still refer to it as an unusual year for the production of cotton. The following year, 1840, witnessed the establishment of an excellent literary institution at Evergreen, which has ever since been known as the Evergreen Academy. Suitable steps had been taken the year previous to locate the institution at the point where it now stands, but not until 1840 was it formally opened for the matriculation of students. Prior to this time little or no business was conducted in the now thrifty town of Evergreen, and it appears that up to this period the community boasted of no other name than that of Corsey's Old Field. When, however, such men as Rev. Alexander Travis, J. V. Perryman, James Tomlinson, Garland Goode, Nicholas Stallworth, Churchill Jones, Nathan Godbold, Chesley Crosby, John Crosby, Blanton P. Box, and others, combined their energies and wisdom and determined to establish a literary institution of high merit at this point, the unclassical name of Corsey's Old Field was displaced by the more elegant designation of Evergreen. Mr. Perryman having modestly declined having the place named "Perryville," in honor of himself, as was justly suggested by some one, Rev. Mr. Travis thought that a name might be derived from the verdant foliage that abounded, suggested that the place was *forever green*—meaning to refer, however, *only* to the foliage! The uniqueness of the name struck those most interested in the enterprise, and hence the academy was called Evergreen. The resolutions originally adopted provided for the election of a President and Vice-President of a board of twelve trustees. Rev. Alexander Travis was chosen President, Hon. Churchill Jones, Vice-President, and the following were the original Board of Trustees of the Academy: John D. Travis, Nicholas Stallworth, Littleberry Chapman, James Tomlinson, C. H. Stallworth, Mabry Thomas, Chesley Crosby, John G. Smith, Wilson Ashley, Mason L. Mosely, Garland Goode and Nathan Godbold. An efficient Principal and Assistant were immediately chosen, and the doors of the new institution were thrown open for the reception of pupils. Rev. Horatio Smith became the first Principal, with Mrs. Smith as his Assistant. The success of the new enterprise more than equalled the most sanguine expectations of its founders, and it was soon discovered to be necessary to increase the force of instruction. Accordingly Professor Stroud was engaged, and later the Faculty was increased by the addition of Mr. A. S. Flowers, and Misses Armstrong and Hitchcock. The merits of the institution speedily became known, and students were matriculated, not only from Conecuh, but from the counties of Butler, Wilcox, Monroe, and Mobile, as well. The school numbered as many as 155 upon its roll at different times. For many years it continued in a thriving condition, the pulpit, the bar, the halls of national legislation, the ranks of the army, as well as many a radiant home in this and surrounding counties, having been contributed to by its classical halls.

Eighteen hundred and forty-one is memorable

as having been a year of remarkable excitement in the county. The chief issue, still, was the currency. Undismayed by past reverses, the Democratic Party renewed its efforts to secure the Representative to the Legislature in the session of 1841. Garland Goode was chosen as the advocate of the principles of Democracy, while Churchill Jones led the opposing Whigs. Public sentiment was stirred to its deepest depths, and the passion for success well nigh bordered on to frenzy. The county resounded from limit to limit with impassioned oratory. Every man was a politician, and the emphasis with which he announced his principles, left no doubt as to the political banner beneath which he served. The contest was again close—just enough so, to tantalize the Democratic hosts and to fire them with a determination to renew the conflict the next year. The Whigs bore off the palm, and Mr. Jones was sent to the Legislature. So acceptable a Representative did he prove, that he was returned for three successive terms. With unabated ardor, however, the Democrats entered the field afresh in 1844, under the leadership of A. W. Jones. The opposite party found a worthy champion in the person of Ransom L. Dean. The contest was again close, but this time the Democrats achieved a victory. This conflict between the two parties continued from year to year, as we shall see as we proceed.

In 1841, a tragedy occurred at Bellville, which, because of its boldness, and premeditated concoction, excited the profoundest indignation in all parts of the county. Two negro men, belonging to Mr. Sandy Puryear, of Monroe, had adroitly arranged to rob and destroy the store of Duncan McIntyre, who was then merchandising at Bellville. They succeeded in entering the house, and after ladening themselves with valuables, they quietly set the house on fire within, coolly mounted their horses, and rode toward home. Investigation and vigilant search for a single trace of the stolen goods seemed, for a time, fruitless—and, perhaps, the criminals would have escaped undetected, had not one of the villains undertaken to barter a fine gold watch for a gun. This furnished a clew to the mystery; the advantage was improved, and soon the guilt was fixed upon the scoundrels. After trial, they were duly executed by being hanged, at Monroeville, the following year.

In January, 1844, the first tannery ever established in Conecuh was built near Bellville, under the auspices of Messrs. J. R. Hawthorne and John H. Farnham. For a number of years it continued in a flourishing condition, as it furnished leather to Conecuh and to citizens in counties adjoining.

It was by no means an uncommon occurrence, at this period, to see slave speculators plying their trade as they would pass, here and there, into different parts of the country. The slaves were usually transported in wagons; and these dealers would locate themselves, for several days together, at the different centres of population,—pitch their tents,—and exhibit their slaves to all desiring to purchase. It is a matter of public congratulation that the Slave Trade, so fraught with innumerable evils, belongs to the times of the far past.

The following is a list of the different county officers of Conecuh during the period embraced in the foregoing chapter:

COUNTY JUDGES.*

1835—J. V. Perryman.†
1836—Henry F. Stearns.
1841—Benjamin J. Goodloe.
1845—A. W. Jones.‡

SHERIFFS.

1837—William E. Ellis.
1841—David F. Henderson.
1844—William E. Ellis.

CIRCUIT CLERKS.

1837—Churchill Jones. §
1841—Wilson Ashley. ‖
1845—Nicholas Stallworth. ‖‖

---

*Until 1850, the County Judges were elected by the Legislature, with term of service of four years.

†Resigned the next year.

‡Resigned before the expiration of his term.

§It was universally understood that this election was held in the interest of A. D. Cary, who, being Receiver at the Land Office, was legally disqualified to offer for the position, but who could do the work for another.

‖For Mr. Cary.

‖‖For Mr. Cary.

The following is a list of the members of the General Assembly:

SENATORS.

1836—Samuel W. Oliver.
1837—Herndon Lee Henderson.
1839—Stephen S. Andrews.
1842—John Watkins.
1845—John Morrisette.

REPRESENTATIVES.

1835—Wilson Ashley.
1836—Jephtha V. Perryman.
1837—Jephtha V. Perryman.
1838—James M. Bolling.
1839—James M. Bolling.
1840—W. A. Bell.
1841—Churchill Jones.
1842—Churchill Jones.
1843—Churchill Jones.
1844—A. W. Jones.

Chapter XVI.

Chapter of Biography—Hon. J. S. Hunter—Richard Warren, etc.

JOHN STARKE HUNTER

was an attorney of some distinction, who came to Conecuh shortly after it became a county. He was a native of Camden, Kershaw District, S. C. His early literary training was of the first order, having graduated from the South Carolina College. He was admitted to the bar to practice law in 1816, and two or three years later turned his face westward toward Alabama, the fame of whose inviting territory had already reached the older States. He first located at Claiborne, in Monroe county, as the law partner of Hon. A. P. Bagby. Thence he removed to Sparta, and became the partner of Samuel W. Oliver. About the year 1829 he removed from Conecuh to Hayneville, Lowndes county, where he continued the practice of law. In 1834 he was promoted, by election, to the circuit judgeship to succeed Hon. John W. Paul, but remained upon the bench only a single year. In 1836 he was placed upon the electoral ticket for Martin Van Buren. In 1840 he was sent from the county of Lowndes to the Legislature, and after a single year's service in this branch of the General Assembly, he was elected Senator. Resigning his seat in the Senate in 1843, he removed to Dallas county. While residing in Cahaba, he combined planting with the practice of law. In 1849 he was again summoned to the arena of politics to join in a contest with Hon. S. W. Harris for Congressional honors. In this contest his opponent was successful. He removed from Dallas county to Kentucky in 1857, and there engaged in raising stock. After an absence of eight years, he returned to Dallas county, Alabama; and during the latter part of 1865, he was elected to the Constitutional Convention. This closed his public career. During the year 1866 he died at Louisville, Kentucky, having completed "three score and ten years." Judge Hunter is described as having been an orator of more than ordinary ability. His manner was easy, his diction chaste, and his reasoning forceful. He was rather austere in his general bearing, which operated sadly against his popularity. In the counties of Dallas and Mobile many of his descendants are still residing.

RICHARD WARREN.*

Maj. Richard Warren removed from Burke county, Georgia, to Alabama in 1817. He first improved a home near Burnt Corn, during the most troublous period of the county's history. Ever careful for the rights and interests of others, he, with true chivalric spirit, erected a fort near Burnt Corn, as a refuge against the depredations of the Indians. After a sojourn of one year here, he removed southward, and

---

*The author regrets his inability to secure no fuller record of the life and services of this honored and useful citizen.

was the first to venture across Murder creek, and to erect a home on the eastern side. He settled the place now owned by the Messrs. William and John Burgamy. Mr. Warren and his sons were the first white inhabitants who lived in the neighborhood of Sparta.

JOHN GREENE, SR.,

came to Conecuh county as early as 1816. At that time it was embraced within the broad limits of Monroe. He was born in Abbeville District, South Carolina, on March 8th, 1790. When he had attained to ten years of age, his father removed with his family to Jackson county, Georgia, where he resided till 1816. Coming to Conecuh at this period, Mr. Greene found it without the slightest trace of civilization. But, thoroughly prepared to grapple with the difficulties here encountered, he began to establish his home in the midst of the wild forests. Quite fortunate for upper Conecuh, and for its educational interests, one of its first citizens was a man whose attention had been largely directed to literary pursuits. Of course, at this period of the country's history, educational facilities were exceedingly meagre. According to Mr. Greene's own statement, he was indebted, for his acquirements, to a small public library in Jackson county, Georgia. Here, under the direction of a judicious friend, he was enabled to pursue a course of reading, and to improve his handwriting. Ambitious of future eminence, he prosecuted with zeal his studies to the utmost of his facilities, and finally decided to adopt the profession of teaching. He was the first to establish a school in Conecuh, and has trained for usefulness many of her best and honored citizens. At different times, Mr. Greene has had accorded him by his fellow-citizens, worthy honors. Twice has he been selected as her Representative in the General Assembly of the State—once in 1824 and again in 1828. Though a Union man, he was chosen to represent Conecuh in the Secession Convention in 1861; and in 1875, was sent as a delegate to the Constitutional Convention. Coming to Conecuh in early manhood, with no other resources at command than an honest heart, a courageous energy, and an unbending will, he has accumulated a fortune, reared a useful family, and by his sage counsel and public-spiritedness, has aided largely in advancing the interests of the county from its organization to the present. He is one of the very few persons now alive who has lived under the administration of every President, from Washington to Arthur. Venerable with age, Mr. Greene still lives in the midst of his fellow citizens, honored and revered by all who know him.

J. RICHARD HAWTHORNE

is a native of Robinson county, North Carolina, where he was born March 8th, 1805. Five years later, his father removed, with his family, to Wilkinson county, Georgia. Here the family resided until 1817, when they removed to Conecuh county. The first place of permanent residence was near the home of the late

Henry Stanley, now in the beautiful little village of Bellville. Here was pitched the family tent when Richard was a bright boy of twelve summers. At the time of the settlement of this locality it was known as "The Ponds"—a name derived from the extensive lakes which lay to the east of the community. Highly gifted with native powers, mental and physical, Mr. Hawthorne's influence was felt as he advanced toward the period of manhood's perfect mould. He was equal to the hardships incident to a frontier section, and from straitened circumstances he rose to the possession of considerable wealth. In 1837 Mr. Hawthorne was the nominee of his (the Democratic) party, against a very formidable opponent, Jephtha V. Perryman. And though he belonged to the minority party of the county, his popularity came well nigh securing for him the laurels of the contest. For when the ballots were counted he came within seven votes of victory. No man who has ever lived in Conecuh exerted a broader or more wholesome influence, than did J. Richard Hawthorne. His zeal in all matters relating to the public weal was proverbial. He occupied several positions of public trust before his removal to another section. In 1854 he removed to Pine Apple, Wilcox county. Here his influence was not inactive, and soon public appreciation summoned him to active usefulness. He was sent to represent the county in two terms of the Legislature, and has been frequently called upon to act in matters requiring calm and dispassionate consideration. He has reared a large and respectable family, and accumulated considerable property. He still lives to wield a godly influence in the promotion of the general good. Generous, hospitable as a prince, warm-hearted and public-spirited, and above all, a devout Christian gentleman, his usefulness is destined to be commensurate with his days.

JEPHTHA V. PERRYMAN,

to whom reference has been had several times in the progress of this history, was born in Twiggs county, Georgia, February 9th, 1798. Thence he removed to Henry county, and after his marriage to Miss Jones, he removed to Conecuh, and erected a home on the west side of Murder creek, opposite the present site of Evergreen. He was among the first judges of the county court, having occupied this position as early as 1835. After serving the county one year in the administration of justice, he resigned, and became the Whig candidate for the Legislature. He was the Representative of the county for two successive terms, during which time he was efficient in aiding the State to pass through the financial storm that was sweeping the country. This ended his activity in public life for a number of years. In 1858 or 1859 he was made the superintendent of education for the county. And again did he re-enlist, with all the ardor of his nature, in the promotion of public improvements. The projected railroad from Montgomery to Pensacola fired his enthusiasm and enlisted his activity to the utmost tension. Not only did he liberally contribute of his purse to the undertaking, but engaged as one of the contractors to build the road, and it is thought undue exposure, incidental to his work, produced sickness, and finally death, which took place at his home, on March 30th, 1861—just a few days prior to the completion of the two ends of the road. Judge Perryman was the embodiment of a positive nature. He lived in an atmosphere entirely above the reach of the petty arts with which politicians sometimes seek to woo the masses. If convinced of the correctness of a given course of conduct, the force of public opinion was as weak as the breath of the zephyr. He was firm, without being obstinate; positive, without being stern. To him the town of Evergreen is largely indebted. His earnest spirit gave life to many of its first improvements. He was notably identified with the establishment of the academy in the town. The same ardency that fired his zeal whenever he addressed his energy to an undertaking, gave a glow to his patriotism at the sound of the tocsin of war. When Lincoln was declared elected, Judge Perryman tendered, by telegraph, to Gov. A. B. Moore—then the Chief Executive of the State—his two sons and five thousand dollars. The beauty that invested his useful life was, that whatever he undertook, he did it without ostentation. Duty was his pole-star, and not the opinions of his fellows. He is described as having been exceedingly liberal and hospitable. "No petty avarice, no sordid ambition, characterized a single act of his life, and whatever fault may have been imputed to him, no one thought him capable of a dishonorable act." In the bosom of his family, and surrounded by his friends, he died at home, and was interred on the Franklin Plantation—the burial ground of his father-in-law, William Jones, Sr. Within a short distance of his first home in Conecuh, his dust is slumbering to-day.

SAMUEL BURNETT

came to Conecuh and located at Hampden Ridge as early as 1820. His native State was Georgia, where he was born in the year 1777. Mr. Burnett was the possessor of such elements of character as made him conspicuous among his fellow citizens. Quite social in his disposition, jocular and hospitable, and withal, the possessor of considerable executive ability, he was remarkably popular. As a result, he had been a resident of the county only ten years, when he was chosen judge of the county court. In this honored capacity he served Conecuh for two successive terms. During the terms of service as county judge, he would go from his home, on Hampden Ridge, to the court house, at Sparta, every day and return. An anecdote is related of him, as connected with one of his trips from the court house to his home, and as illustrative of his confidence in his favorite steed, as well as of the exuberance of his humor, even under trying circumstances. According to his daily habit, he left his office, at Sparta, late one afternoon, in mid-winter, and though he knew the swollen condition of Murder creek, and that the waters had swept away the bridge, he resolved to cross the dangerous stream and reach Hampden Ridge before night. Some friends, after endeavoring to dissuade him from such a mad-cap purpose, followed closely after him as soon as his departure had been ascertained. To their dismay, they found, on reaching the deep stream, that he had been swept from his horse, and had succeeded in clutching hold of the trunk of a magnolia that was projecting into the waters. Astride this, with his body of 225 pounds, avoirdupois, going upward and downward, with the see-saw motion of the huge log, he was first beheld by the anxious eyes of his friends. In response to the question, "What are you doing up there, Judge?" he replied, "Ah, gentlemen, I'm navigating!" In his business relations Judge Burnett is said to have been scrupulously exact, spurning the thought of indebtedness to any one, and positively forbidding any one to owe him. He was the parent of eight children, most of whom lived in Conecuh, and themselves reared families of influence. John D. Burnett, Esq., a young attorney, of Evergreen, and among the most promising young men of the county, is a grandson of Judge Samuel Burnett. The subject of this sketch died at his old home, on Hampden Ridge, in 1839.

HENRY FRANKLIN STEARNS.

About the year 1830 there came to Conecuh a young Canadian, of pleasant address, and with a liberal education. A stranger amid strangers, he is said to have spent a night at the home of Alexander Autrey, on Hampden Ridge. Mr. Autrey, having learned that he was a young man just beginning his rough encounters with the world, and having been pleased with the unusual promise couched in the elegant gentleman, and more with his pronounced principles of Universalism, gave him some substantial aid, and rendered him valuable service in securing his introduction into Conecuh. This young man was the subject of this sketch. Henry Franklin Stearns was born in the county of Stanstead, Dominion of Canada, province of Ontario, on March 21st, 1805. He was of English parentage. He was graduated from a college in New Brunswick. In 1830 he came to Conecuh, and found employment in teaching a school for some time near Bellville. Shortly after this he addressed himself to the study of the law, and was admitted to practice in 1834 or 1835. At that time ample scope was afforded him for the exercise of his legal powers, and he entered at once upon a successful practice. He had continued his practice but about two years, however, when he was appointed judge of the county court. Judge Stearns was noted for his invincible zeal. In him every cause which he espoused found an ardent advocate. By discreet management he accumulated a respectable property. The hospitable spirit, so characteristic of the well-to-do residents of Conecuh, was entirely congenial with Judge Stearns when he became a citizen of the county. At one time he was the candidate of his (the Whig) party for Representative in the General Assembly; and though his party was in the majority in the county, he sustained defeat. This was due, however, to the fact that he was of Northern birth. He was honored with being a delegate to the National Whig Convention which nominated Henry Clay for the Presidency. At the time of his death, Judge Stearns had in course of successful prosecution a plan for the establishment of a cotton factory at Fowler's Mills. His waning health forbade the execution of a work, which, had it been successful, would have conferred lasting benefits upon the county at large. In 1856 he went to Texas in the interest of a plantation in that State. Returning home during the following year, he was able to get no nearer than Claiborne, Monroe county, where he died, on February 3rd, 1857. Here, too, was the resting place of his remains.

JOHN BELL

came to Conecuh about 1819. He was an emigrant from Ireland. At the time of his removal to this county, Bellville, then called "The Ponds," was one of the most prominent settlements in Conecuh. He is said to have been quiet, unobtrusive and enterprising. The vast ponds which bound the community on the east, he determined to drain—and accordingly dug a ditch of great length and considerable depth, which crosses the road just below Bellville. In honor of John Bell the beautiful village was finally named. The time of his death is not known. He sleeps beneath the sod, under a wide-spreading tree, near the home of Mrs. Stanley.

CHAPTER XVII.

Conecuh from 1845 to 1855—Status of the County at this Period—Acrimonious Politics—Sad Tragedy—Steam Navigation of Conecuh—A Disaster and a Protracted Law Suit—Caterpillars—Mexican War—Sickness in the County, &c.

This period introduces us into the midst of stirring scenes. By its increased facilities the county was now brought into easy communication with the world beyond. A new generation of men had been reared upon her soil, and were coming rapidly to the front, to the assumption of the control of affairs,—men who were in sympathy with the over-reaching strides of advancement now being made in all departments.

The fertile lands of Conecuh, and their prodigious yield, had drawn industry and capital from various directions, until now the population of Conecuh had reached almost ten thousand. Business, in all its branches, was thriving,—and many of the citizens of the county were becoming immensely wealthy. The indications of prosperity were evident in the elegant homes, the extensive plantations—tilled now by numerous slaves—the comfortable "negro quarters," the neatly built churches and school houses, and the magnificent equipages of many of the wealthiest families. What a transformation had been produced in the county within a period of three and a half decades! The hand of Industry had made the wilderness to blossom as the rose.

But that which was engrossing more and more public attention was, the political issues of the period. The alternating victories secured by both parties kept them constantly on the alert. The greatest care had to be taken to avoid the mistake of placing any other in the field than the most popular man. The standard bearer of the Democratic hosts in the county, in 1845, was James A. Stallworth; that of the Whigs was Mortimer Boulware. Mr. Stallworth was a young man, who was just now catching public attention by the brilliancy of his oratory, and by the readiness with which he grappled with the issues of his opponents. He found in Mr. Boulware a formidable opponent. The county was never more thoroughly canvassed and aroused. Everywhere the zealous candidates were met by vast crowds. In the election which followed, both parties strained their facilities to the utmost tension. Mr. Stallworth bore off the palm of victory, and thus commenced a brilliant political career, as will be seen in the future history of the county.

In March of this year, a sad tragedy occurred in the vicinity of Bellville, which, because of its connection with one of the most distinguished families of Conecuh, cast a gloom over the whole county. A freedman, who was popularly known as "Free Henry," in a rencounter with Joshua and James Hawthorne—two sons of Col. J. R. Hawthorne—fatally stabbed the latter named young man. The freedman was arrested, lodged in jail, at Sparta, at the approaching term of court convicted of murder, and was publicly executed by hanging, in October of the same year.

The success which had constantly attended the navigation of the Conecuh by raft boats, excited a desire finally to launch upon her waters a more stately craft, and one in more apt keeping with modern advancement. Accordingly a meeting was called at Brooklyn, in August, 1845, to consider the feasibility of undertaking the navigation of the river by steam. It was called the Steam Navigation Meeting. It was the occasion of much interest, many of the wealthiest and most enterprising gentlemen of the county having responded to the call. The advisability of such an enterprise was duly considered, and a stock company was formed. Subsequently the steamer "Shaw" was purchased, duly manned, and started on a trip up the river. Expectations became more sanguine still, when the steamer had reached Brooklyn landing without hindrance or disaster. The boat, unloaded of its cargo of supplies, which it had borne up the stream from Pensacola, was re-loaded with cotton, and, amid the most jubilant expectations, started southward. But, alas! when it had descended the stream but a short distance, it struck an unfriendly snag and was sunk, and with it sank the hopes of the ardent instigators of the enterprise. The whole cargo was lost. Mr. George Turk—the father of Laban Turk, of Monroe—was the principal loser, having on board most of the cotton. The result of this sad catastrophe was a protracted law suit between Mr. Turk and the stock company, which terminated in favor of the plaintiff. Thus ended all efforts to propel boats, by steam, upon the Conecuh river. This enhanced the value of Claiborne, Monroe county, for it was now the most accessible shipping and receiving point to the planters and merchants of Conecuh.

A sudden check was placed upon the prosperity of the county in 1846, by the destruction of the cotton by the caterpillar. So sudden and wide-spread were the ravages of the cotton worm, that the crop of that year came well nigh proving a failure. During this year, too, there was an alarming prevalence of pneumonia in Conecuh. It spread with violence in all portions of the county, and did not cease its ravages for several years together. The year 1846 is memorable in the annals of the country as the beginning of hostilities between the United States and Mexico. During the latter part of this year several victories had been achieved by General Taylor. When the news of bloodshed, and his splendid successes, reached the States, crowds of volunteers demanded the acceptance of their services. Nor did the patriotism of the Conecuhians lie dormant, while others, from different sections, were rallying beneath the American banner. It is to be regretted that the names of but two of the brave patriots of Conecuh, who enlisted in this war, can be secured. These are William R. King and Mark Travis. The former of these died in service in Mexico, and his remains were sent home and interred in the graveyard at Bellville. Mr. Travis survived the war, and returned to his home, bearing the mark of a wound received in the battle of Cherubusco.

The only interest which attaches to the history of the county for several years together, subsequent to the period already adverted to, is that which gathers around the political contests. The Democratic Party, having been led to victory in 1845, under the leadership of their young champion, James A. Stallworth, continued to hold the majority of the popular vote until 1849. At this period the Whigs nominated William A. Ashley as their candidate for legislative honors. Through personal popularity, as an able advocate of the principles of the Whig Party, Mr. Ashley succeeded in securing triumph to his party, and marked distinction to himself. This was to him the beginning of a very long and popular career as a leader in Conecuh. Such was his acceptance during his term of service, that he was rewarded by his party with a second nomination and was again elected by the popular voice of the county. Political supremacy was held now by the Whigs until 1857. For after Mr. Ashley had been elected State Senator, Andrew Jay became the favored leader of the party, by which he was honored with two successive terms of office in the lower house of the General Assembly.

With 1854 came the first railroad excitement ever experienced by the people of Conecuh. Prodigious advantages were promised the people of the county if they would only aid in the construction of the Mobile and Girard Railroad. Eloquent agents depicted in glowing description, the advantages which must accrue to the county by the projected enterprise, and thus succeeded in booking handsome subscriptions from very many of the citizens. The total failure to reap any benefits from the road, bred dissatisfaction and gave rise to serious litigation, which resulted in the recovery of a portion of the funds contributed to the establishment of the enterprise. A comparative lull of several years followed this period.

The following is a list of county officers who served during the decade included between 1845 and 1855:

COUNTY JUDGES.

1849—P. D. Castillo.*

PROBATE JUDGES.

1850—A. D. Cary.

SHERIFFS.

1847—John D. Travis.†
1848—William M. Stallworth.‡
1851—Stephen Richardson.
1854—George Christian.

CIRCUIT CLERKS.

1849—Mark B. Travis.
1855—Mark B. Travis.

---

*Appointed to fill an unexpired term. The following year the office was abolished.
†Resigned the following year.
‡Appointed.

COUNTY CLERKS.

1837—1841—Jordan B. Lewis.*
1841—1845—John D. Cary.
1845—1849—John D. Cary.
1849—1850—Sherman G. Forbes.†

SENATORS.

1847—John Morrisett.
1851—William Perry Leslie.
1853—William A. Ashley.

REPRESENTATIVES.

1845—James A. Stallworth.
1847—James A. Stallworth.
1849—William A. Ashley.
1851—William A. Ashley.
1853—Andrew Jay.
1855—Andrew Jay.

---

*This should have been embodied in the earlier list, but was overlooked.

†Office universally abolished in 1850 throughout the State.

Chapter XVIII.

A Chapter of Biography—John Crosby—James M. Bolling—Rev. Hanson Lee, etc.

JOHN CROSBY.

Among the best and noblest of the citizens of Conecuh, during his career, was John Crosby. He came to the county from Chester District, South Carolina, in 1832, and settled, first, at the home owned at present by Dr. John D. Reilly. In personal appearance, Mr. Crosby was rather tall, of dignified mien, with ruddy complexion, and hair of raven blackness. In character, he was exceedingly firm and positive. Possessed of a vigorous energy and an unconquerable will, he bore down before him all difficulties, and rarely failed of success in any pursuit. If he was fond of accumulating wealth, he was equally fond of bestowing it upon any object that commended itself to his heart and judgment. While he was proverbially liberal, he grew wealthy within a few years; thereby exemplifying the sacred expression, "The liberal soul shall be made fat." Commencing with resources quite meagre, he had amassed a respectable fortune in twenty-five years. During this period he had become the owner of two extensive plantations, well manned with negro slaves. To the comfort of these slaves he was devoted with a tenderness quite unusual. He was universally esteemed for his piety, and manifested his devotion to the cause of Sacred Truth by being one of the most consistent of the members of the Baptist Church, at Bellville, for quite a number of years. A characteristic anecdote is related of him, as illustrative of his thorough honesty, and abiding conviction of right. During a given session of the Circuit Court, held at Sparta, Mr. Crosby was one of the petit jurors. In that capacity he would serve during the day, and after adjournment, ride to his home in the neighborhood of Bellville. Rising with the earliest tinge of dawn, he would start each morning toward Sparta, going *via* one of his plantations to give directions to his laborers for the day. One morning he was unduly detained at his farm, and did not appear at the court house until after his name had been called, his absence announced, and a forfeiture entered against him by the presiding Judge. Coming into the court room, he was apprised of the imposition of the fine. He was summoned into the presence of the court to give the reason of his absence. He replied that his absence was due to the protracted attention which he had to bestow that morning upon his affairs at his plantation. Whereupon the court asked him if any reason could be assigned by himself why the forfeiture should not be entered against him. He very frankly replied: "Oh, no! I have no excuse whatever. The whole matter is just as it should be. The fine is justly imposed." An example of his liberality is found in the fact that he donated to Howard College one thousand dollars, and defrayed the expenses of a theological student throughout his entire course. After a useful and exemplary career, he died at his beautiful home near Bellville, in the early part of 1849.

JAMES M. BOLLING.

This gentleman made his *debut* into public life in 1838, when he represented Conecuh in the Legislature. Though young, he soon became one of the most active members of the General Assembly. Such was the pleasantness of his demeanor, that he became a favorite among the members. He was returned to the Legislature for two successive terms. From the beginning, he gave promise of distinction at the bar. He married a daughter of the Hon. Reuben Saffold, Judge of the Supreme Court; after which he removed to Hayneville, Lowndes county, where he continued to practice to the close of his life.

REV. HANSON LEE

removed, with the remainder of his father's family, to Conecuh, in the earliest settlement of the county. He was the sixth son of Joel Lee. The subject of the present memoir was born in Johnston county, North Carolina, on December 27th, 1816. He was a young man of brilliant parts, and at an early age resolved to fit himself, through self-training, for future usefulness. By dint of close and laborious study, he succeeded in acquiring a classical education of a high order of merit. Recognizing his ability, the college at Marysville Tennessee, conferred upon him the degree of A.

M. When he was a lad of sixteen he was baptized by Rev. Alexander Travis, and became a member of the famous Old Bethany Church. He was ordained to preach the gospel about 1844. In connection with preaching, he adopted the profession of teacher. His services were secured at different points as teacher. His first school was at Brooklyn. Thence he was invited to take a school in Lee county, Georgia, whence he removed to Louisiana. Here he became the President of Mount Lebanon College. In connection with his duties here, as Professor, he became the editor of the *Louisiana Baptist*—the organ of the Baptist denomination in Louisiana for a number of years. He died at his home in 1862. In writing his obituary, Rev. William Carey Crane, D. D., LL. D., President of Baylor University, Texas, said: "A great man in Israel has fallen."

THOMAS W. SIMPSON

was a native of South Carolina. He was born March 23rd, 1806. Coming to Conecuh, together with his father, as early as 1818, he enjoyed but few educational advantages. He commenced life in circumstances quite humble, with no other reliance than a strong determination and a heroic energy. With the growing development of the county he continued to increase his acquisitions until he had surrounded himself with a property quite respectable. Mr. Simpson was one of the most useful, and yet one of the most modest, of Conecuh's citizens. He delighted in dispensing hospitality. His roof was the refuge of many a way-worn traveler. To a praiseworthy degree he exemplified the principles which he professed as Mason, Son of Temperance, and Christian. Among his children who survive him is Ransom Simpson, of Snow Hill, Wilcox county—a citizen whose worth is greatly prized in his adopted county. Mr. Simpson died at his home, near Bellville, June 1st, 1861.

NICHOLAS STALLWORTH, JR.

Prominent among the first generation of young men, reared in Conecuh, was he whose name is recorded at the head of this sketch. He was born in Edgefield District, South Carolina, on February 21st, 1810. When he was only eight years of age he was brought, with the remainder of his father's family, to Alabama. He was married to Miss Martha Travis—eldest daughter of Rev. Alexander Travis. The result of this union was seven children, among whom were Robert P. Stallworth and Frank M. Stallworth, of Falls county, Texas; Major Nick Stallworth, late of Hilliard's Legion; and Mrs. Barnett,* wife of Hon. Samuel A. Barnett, now of Mobile. Reared in the midst of circumstances unfavorable to his mental development, at a time when few or no schools existed, Mr. Stallworth had to depend almost altogether upon self-training. He was lacking in none of the virtues that make a sterling citizen. Hospitable, liberal and

---

*Who died several years ago.

possessed of public spiritedness, he was quite popular with the masses. Without himself seeking the position, he was at one time made Circuit Clerk of Conecuh county. When, in 1850, the office of Judge of Probate was made elective, he warmly espoused the candidacy of A. D. Cary. As early as 1838, Mr. Stallworth foresaw the struggle which reached its bloody culmination in 1861. The tendency of existing political issues caused him to predict the dismemberment of the Union, and the probable abolition of American slavery. Mr. Stallworth died in 1853, in the prime of manhood.

A. D. CARY.

Armstead Dudley Cary was born in Gloucester county, Virginia, October 23rd, 1791. Eight years later his father removed to Clarke county, Georgia, and settled near the famous educational seat of Athens. When he had attained his eleventh year, young Armstead was sent from the paternal roof to receive his elementary training in the famous Waddell High School, in Abbeville District, South Carolina. Here he was the school-fellow of such men as James L. Pettigrew, of South Carolina, and of Governor Lumpkin and Judge A. B. Longstreet, of Georgia. Having been thoroughly fitted here for his future course in college, he returned to his home at Athens, entered the State University, and was graduated in 1813. He at once chose the profession of teacher, and became the principal of a school in Sumter District, South

Carolina. Among his pupils in this school was the Hon. James E. Belser, who, in after years, was a resident of Montgomery, Alabama. Lured by the fascinating descriptions given of the lovely region of the Southwest, Mr. Cary, in 1820, removed to Claiborne, in Monroe county. Here he remained only one year. In 1821 he removed to Bellville, and two years later still, to Sparta. During this time, and for several years subsequent to 1823, he was engaged in teaching. In 1826 he was chosen Clerk of the Circuit Court for Conecuh, which office he held, uninterruptedly, for almost a quarter of a century. In 1833 President Jackson appointed him Receiver of the Land Office for the Sparta District. From this position he was removed in 1850, by President Taylor, because of the fact that he was a Democrat.

Such was the solidity of his character, that Mr. Cary passed through all these eventful scenes with unsullied record. He spurned with derision any proposition that did not fully comport with the principles of rectitude, and strove to shun even "the appearance of evil." The following anecdote is related of him:

As Receiver, he was legally required to make quarterly returns. At the conclusion of one quarter he deposited the enormous sum of $140,000. Just prior to rendering in his returns, he was confidentially advised by a prominent and professional citizen of the county to pay his bondsmen the full amount of the bond of $40,000, and to put the balance in his pocket. Mr. Cary very frankly said: "But that would be dishonest." He was assured that this was the course adopted by nearly all the officers of the department. But Mr. Cary, with characteristic gravity, said: "My code of ethics will not permit me to do so dishonorable an act." And the amount was forthwith deposited.

For many years he combined the offices of Receiver and Circuit Clerk. He was enabled to do this in the face of a prohibitory statute, by some friend securing the office for him, by securing his own election and appointing Mr. Cary as his deputy. Valuable service was rendered him in this way by Churchill Jones, Wilson Ashley, and Nicholas Stallworth, Jr. Such was the personal and professional popularity of Mr. Cary, that all efforts to defeat him before the people were totally unavailing. After the establishment of the Probate Court in the county, in 1850, Mr. Cary became the first Judge of Probate. In September of that year he became a member of the Baptist denomination, and was baptized by Elder Alexander Travis.

During the closing years of his life, Mr. Cary was tenderly cared for in the homes of his children. His earthly career terminated on December 7th, 1879. No man who has ever lived in Conecuh has left a fairer record than Judge Cary. He was universally recognized as a man who was swayed in life by the purest motives. So circumspect was his deportment in all relations, that no one has ever ventured to cast any asperities upon his fair name.

WILLIAM BARRETT TRAVIS, THE HERO OF THE "ALAMO."

Near the ancient Spanish town of San Antonio, and on the left bank of the stream of the same name, in the southern border of Texas, is to be seen, to-day, a cluster of block-houses. This is the famous site of Fort Alamo, the calm bravery of whose ill-starred defenders entitles them to a place in the world's history along-side that of the heroes of Marathon and Thermopylæ. At this sacred spot, baptized in fire and blood, was displayed a heroism unsurpassed in the annals of conflict. Around this little spot centres the thrill of the War for Texan Independence.

William Barrett Travis was born in Edgefield District, South Carolina, (near Old Fort Ninety-Six,) on August 9th, 1809. He was the son of Mark Travis, Sr., and nephew to Elder Alexander Travis. The family removed to the county of Conecuh in 1818, and founded a home that is near the location of the present home of Rev. Andrew Jay. Young Travis was as thoroughly educated as the educational facilities of a frontier region would allow. When he reached maturity, he studied for the bar, at Claiborne, under Hon. James Dellett. Whether induced by the rapid developments made in the far West, to remove to Texas, or whether led by love of adventure, is not known. But, quite early in 1835, we find him bidding farewell to his quiet home in South Alabama and removing to Texas. When he reached the province, he found it in a state of seething excitement. The rapid strides which were being made by Santa Anna toward centralization met with a warm protest from the Texans. Young, ardent and chivalrous, Mr. Travis was soon in profound sympathy with the Texan patriots. In the very beginning of hostilities, we find him conspicuous as a chosen leader. When, at length, a declaration of hostilities was made by Santa Anna against the Anglo-American Rebels of Texas, and when, at the head of an army of 4,000, he marched upon San Antonio, near the beginning of 1836, we find Col. W. B. Travis in command at this point. The advance of Santa Anna's army reached the heights of the Alazan, overlooking the city of San Antonio, on the morning of the 22nd of February. Before so formidable a force as that led by the Mexican President, Colonel Travis retired with 144 men to the Alamo. Upon the occupation of the city, Santa Anna sent a summons to the garrison to surrender. The response of the heroic Travis was a cannon shot from the battery,—for he too well knew the treachery and blood-thirstiness of his foe. Travis had within the fort fourteen cannon, but only a limited supply of ammunition. Having received so defiant a reply from the American commander, Santa Anna caused to be run up above the church of the city a blood-red flag, proclaiming, "*No Quarter!*"

On the 24th, Travis dispatched couriers to San Felipe and Goliad for assistance. Meanwhile the Mexicans steadily bombarded the fort without effect. At quite an early hour on the morning of the 25th, the

Mexicans evinced a more determined spirit than ever. They brought into active play all their available guns. Toward noon Santa Anna left his headquarters in the city, crossed the river, and gave his personal supervision to the well directed aim of the gunners. Wherever he could screen himself from view, he would advance and plant his guns nearer the walls of the fort. To prevent surprise, the Texans sallied forth on the night of the 25th, and burnt some houses standing near the fort. The following morning a brisk skirmish took place, but without decisive results. The overwhelming numbers of the Mexicans were now greatly increased, and Santa Anna proceeded to draw the toils of his strength more closely around the walls of the besieged fort, in order to cut off the garrison from water. But in this he signally failed. When night had again settled upon the assailants and the assailed, Travis's men made another sortie, and again destroyed some houses, behind which the besieging forces might take refuge. For several days together the Mexicans continued the bombardment without the accomplishment of any serious results.

On March 2nd, the garrison in the Alamo was reinforced by thirty-two citizen soldiers, who had cut their way through the ranks of the enemy. These were under the command of the gallant Capt. John W. Smith, of Gonzales. On the day following Colonel Travis sent a courier to Washington, where the State Convention was assembled, and with the following message:

"I am still here, in fine spirits, and well-to-do. With 145 men, I have held this place ten days against a force variously estimated at from 1,500 to 6,000; and I shall continue to hold it until I get relief from my countrymen, or I will perish in its defence. We have had a shower of cannon balls continually falling among us the whole time, yet none of us have fallen. We have been miraculously preserved."

During the day Colonel Bonham, who had been sent to Goliad to secure reinforcements, returned to the fort and united again with his comrades in its defence. After nightfall, the Texans again issued forth upon a sally, but without the achievement of any success. The morning of the 4th of March dawned upon the besiegers and the besieged. Sharp cannonade was renewed by the assailants. The ammunition being scarce within the fort, the garrison but seldom fired. The day wore heavily away, and no change still was produced in the situation.

At night, Santa Anna called a council of war, and urged upon his officers the necessity of a speedy assault upon the fort. Against this suggestion, however, all his officers remonstrated, and counseled tardiness until the siege guns should arrive. But the impetuous President had grown impatient of delay already. Given to celerity of movement, he chafed under the worrying delay incident to a siege. His wish finally prevailed. He had resolved upon storming the fort. It was to be attacked simultaneously from different directions by four columns under the leadership of his most experienced officers. The orders of the commander-in-chief were given with the utmost minuteness. Each column was to be provided with scaling ladders, pickaxes and crowbars. The signal of attack was to be given precisely at midnight. The cavalry was to be marshalled in the rear to prevent the desertion of the unwilling troops, and to intercept the escape of the Americans. For some reason the time of attack was delayed several hours. At precisely 4 o'clock on the morning of March 6th—the thirteenth day of the siege—the bugle sounded the attack along the whole Mexican line, and a firm, onward movement was made. The garrison soon became aware of the situation, and leaped to their guns, and poured upon their assailants a storm of lead and iron. Before the well directed fire of the Texans the three columns on the north, west and east staggered and swung back. Some confusion was produced by several columns becoming commingled; but the solid mass rallied again under efficient officers, and renewed with vigor the assault. This time they succeeded in effecting an entrance into the wall of the yard running around the fort. About the same time the column advancing from the south made a breach in the wall, and captured one of the guns. This cannon was commanded by Colonel Travis himself, and it is supposed that he fell early in the action, as he was found dead very near the gun. The Mexicans turned this favorite gun upon the last remaining stronghold, and dislodged the Texans, who took refuge in the different buildings of the enclosure.

The conflict now began in good earnest. Each building was a separate battle scene. Resolved to die with as much profit as possible to the struggling province, every man fought like a bayed tiger. When the enemy would press so closely upon one that he could not load his piece, he would reverse his gun and club every advancing assailant until he fell pierced with a bullet, or driven through with a bayonet. The heroic Crockett, knowing that death was inevitable, struck down his enemies until, when his corpse was found, it was in the centre of a circling heap of dead Mexicans. Colonel Bowie was confined to his bed in the last stage of consumption. As the enemy rushed into his room, he sat upright in his bed, and killed several of the foe before he himself was killed. The details of the horrible massacre have oftentimes been given, and need not be repeated here. It may be proper to state, however, that the bodies of the Texans were collected into heaps and burned. A year later, Col. John N. Seguin superintended the collection and proper interment of the bones of these heroes.

As you enter the capitol, at Austin, you are confronted by a monument bearing this inscription: "Thermopylæ had its messenger of defeat; the Alamo had none." Thus went out into the darkness of a horrible death the star of the brilliant and brave Col. William Barrett Travis. With the change of adaptation, we adopt here the language of Albert Pike, in his "Grave of Washington:"

"Disturb not his slumber! Let TRAVIS here sleep,
  'Neath the boughs of the willow that over him weep!
  His arm is unnerved, but his deeds remain bright
  As the stars in the dark-vaulted heaven at night.

"O, wake not the hero! His battles are o'er!
  Let him rest, undisturbed, on Antonio's fair shore!
  On the river's green border as flowery dressed,
    With the hearts he loved fondly, let TRAVIS here rest."

Chapter XIX.

Conecuh from 1855 to 1860—A Period of Stirring Activity—More Progress—Academy at Bellville—Know-Nothingism in Conecuh—A County Organ Established—Railroad Excitement—Telegraphic Line—Murder of Allen Page—Ominous Signs on the Political Horizon.

The period into which we are now introduced far exceeded in importance and excitement any which had preceded it. Rapid and marked changes were being created in the politics of the country by the addition of new elements to the sectional controversies which were agitating the country in all directions. The respective parties in Conecuh, of course, echoed the sentiments of their leaders. It was during this period that the Whig Party ceased to have a national existence. The formation of an Anti-Foreign and No-Popery Party, called the "Know-Nothing Party," blotted from existence the party which had been controlled by the Whigs for a long time. The political contest was no longer between the Whigs and Democrats, as before, but it was now waged beneath the banners of the Democratic and Know-Nothing Parties. In 1855 Maj. Andrew Jay, who had been conspicuous for a number of years before the people of the county, as an ardent worker and wise counselor in political affairs, and who had previously been the Representative of the Whig Party in the Legislature, was chosen as the standard bearer of the new party, and sent again to the General Assembly. But these political contests, so far from retarding the intellectual or material development of the county, were, beyond question, one of the cardinal factors that contributed to the advancement of her people. Eagerness for information relative to the great questions that were now swaying the people of the Union, prompted the increase of political literature in the homes of Conecuh. This, acting in concert with the frequent discussion of these principles on the stump, in the social circle, and in the homes, awakened inquiry and stimulated the mental energy of the youth of the county. And the combination of these concurrent causes, too, led to increased facilities in the county for the transmission of intelligence, and finally, to the encouragement of the establishment of the great thoroughfare which now penetrates the county from north to south.

In 1854 the citizens of Bellville, and the surrounding communities, established an academy in the village, and the following year its doors were thrown open for the reception of pupils. Prof. C. D. Cole was secured as the Principal of the institution, and from the beginning its career has been one of marked prosperity.

The year 1856 witnessed the inauguration of a new enterprise at Sparta—that of the publication of a county organ, under the editorial management of Messrs. Witter and McGinnis. This year, too, gave birth to the agitation of the railroad question. Considerable enthusiasm was awakened by the prospect of having the county favored with the presence of a railroad. Under the impulse of this excitement public meetings were held in different parts of the county. By common consent a sumptuous barbecue was usually had in connection with these occasions. Earnest advocates of the enterprise would unfold the incalculable advantages that would arise from such a thoroughfare; roasted meats and delicate viands would be enjoyed, and then an opportunity would be afforded for subscribing to the establishment of the railroad. An active canvass of the question secured from the county the handsome subscription of $85,000. This liberal subscription secured the location and completion of the road through Conecuh. It may not be amiss, in this connection, to mention the liberal subscribers to whom the county is chiefly indebted for this important line of transportation. The list was headed by the names of Andrew Jay and J. V. Perryman, each of whom subscribed $5,000. Asa Johnson, Elijah McCreary, W. A. Ashley, James A. Stallworth, Caleb Johnson, Y. M. Rabb, M. L. Mosely, Y. S. Hirshfelder, and others, whose names could not be secured, followed with sums ranging from $1,500 to $2,500. Work was commenced soon after from the opposite directions of Montgomery and Pensacola.

In the political contests in the county in 1857 and 1859, the Democrats again attained the supremacy, under the lead of John D. Cary. Elected in 1857 to the General Assembly, he was re-elected to the same position during the following campaign.

In 1858 a telegraphic line of communication was established from Greenville to Mobile. Passing through Conecuh, the enterprising company established an office at Evergreen.

During the following year a brutal tragedy was enacted in Fork Sepulga. Mr. Allen Page, a prominent and highly respected citizen, had started a number of wagons, loaded with cotton, from his gin house, on Tuesday morning, toward Claiborne. In company with Mr. John Wright, Sr., he followed the wagons the next day, in a buggy, and reached Claiborne at night. Having cautiously concealed a gun beneath the cotton in one of the wagons, Irvin Ward accompanied the party until within a short distance of Claiborne, when he separated himself from them, and turned into a road leading to a landing above Claiborne, announcing his purpose to visit some relations living in Clarke county. Before sundering himself from the wagons, however, he informed himself, with the utmost minuteness, with respect to the intention of Messrs. Page and Wright to sell their cotton on Thursday, and to return home on Friday. Having passed beyond the view of the wagons, Ward retraced his steps, hurried back toward his home, and engaged with his brother, Stephen, in the formation of a plot to murder and rob Messrs. Page and Wright upon their return. Accordingly, they placed a small log across the road, on the east side of Little Brewer creek, and within six miles of the home of Mr. Page, in order to check them when they should reach the spot. One of the brothers screened himself behind a pine log, which ran parallel with the road, and in order the more effectually to conceal himself, had stuck here and there, about him, quite a number of gall bushes. The other was secreted about twenty yards to the rear. Both were armed with double-barrel guns. Ere long, the rumbling of the wheels of the buggy was heard, and the murderers lay silently awaiting the favorable moment to fire. The horse reached the log; a short colloquy ensued as to the strange appearance of the log across the road; some doubt was expressed with regard to the inability of the buggy to roll over it, when Mr. Wright proposed to alight and remove it. Just as he had thrown it aside, a load of buckshot was discharged into the bosom of Allen Page, who was seated in the buggy. He instantly threw up his hands and exclaimed, "I am killed," and was in the act of falling from the buggy, when Mr. Wright bounded forward and caught him. Just at this moment another barrel was discharged at Wright, the contents of which did but little execution, as but few shot penetrated his skin. His clothes, however, were sadly perforated by the bullets. It was afterwards ascertained that the most of the load of the second barrel took effect in a root of the log behind which Ward was concealed. Snatching up the lifeless body of Mr. Page, Mr. Wright applied the whip to the excited horse, and dashed up the road at full speed. He left the corpse at the home of Mrs. Bidgood, two miles from the scene of the horrible transaction. In a few hours the community was thoroughly aroused, and excited crowds gathered about the scene of the murder. A pack of negro dogs, belonging to Mr. Jones, was brought into requisition, but were unable to indicate the direction taken by the fugitive murderers. The most intense excitement, mingled with honest indignation, prevailed on all hands. The general reputation of Irvin Ward, coupled with his suspicious conduct on the day preceding the tragedy, led to his arrest. His younger brother, Stephen, was not suspected as being an accomplice, at the time. Irvin Ward was subjected to a rigid examination before Justice K. R. Page. Upon his statement that he had been on a visit to relatives in Clarke county, a runner was sent thither, and it was ascertained that he had not at all visited Clarke. A committee of gentlemen was formed, whose duty it was to ascertain the whereabouts of every man in the community, for several days previous to the murder. The statements of the two brothers, Ward, were found to be false in many essential particulars, and they were seized and held in close custody, until further developments could be made. Finally, after the accumulation of considerable circumstantial evidence against them, they openly confessed themselves to have been the perpetrators of the bloody deed. This confession was made at the home of the deceased, and in the presence of about one hundred auditors. Public notice was now given that they would be hanged the following day at 1 P. M. at the spot where the deed was perpetrated, and just one week subsequent to the bloody transaction. Messengers were dispatched in all directions giving due notice of the proposed execution. Strong guards were placed around the house, and on every approach thereto. A brother of the murderers hastened to Sparta that night, and endeavored to secure the interposition of the sheriff on behalf of the murderers. But he would not interfere. An excited and determined populace had resolved upon the speedy execution of the murderers, and had determined to shoot down any parties who should undertake their rescue. A rude gallows was erected over the spot where the deed was perpetrated, the murderers were marched out in front of about forty citizens and to the place of execution, six miles distant. When they had come near the homes of the Wards, they were met by their relatives—the old parents, brothers and sisters, and the wife of Stephen Ward, bearing in her arms an infant of six weeks. The place of execution was reached, and a statement was made by the murderers. They said that no malice had prompted the bloody deed, for Mr. Page was among their best friends. He had relieved their wants, and those of their families, when their father could not. They had murdered him for the purpose of robbing him of the proceeds of the cotton. After this, the ropes were adjusted by P. D. Page, Esq., and William Wright, and they swung just at 1 o'clock, on Friday, the 18th of November, 1859. When they had ceased to breathe, their bodies were taken in charge by the father and brothers. The sons of Mr. Page, deceased, sent a number of negro men to dig their graves and to assist in a decent interment. At the approaching session of the Circuit Court, bills of indictment were found against about forty of those who were most active in the prosecution and execution of the Wards, and bonds were fixed at $1,000. Judge J. K. Henry, at the next term of the Circuit Court, caused a *nol. pros.* of all the cases, and thus the public mind became quiet upon a subject which had engrossed it for so long a period.

During the same year (1859), successful operations were commenced upon the Montgomery and Pensacola Railroad. From both directions the work began, but the road was not completed until about April, 1861. This is, to-day, one of the most important thoroughfares in all the South. It now constitutes a part of the great line operated under the auspices of the Louisville and Nashville Railroad Company. Entering Conecuh on its northern boundary, it penetrates it southward twenty-four and a half miles.

The year 1860 marks an emphatic era in the political history of the country. Some of the questions which had their birth in the political struggles of former periods, now assumed serious proportions. Grave issues were involved in the coming struggle between the different political organizations of the Union. The acrimony of feeling between the Northern and Southern States, was aggravated by every recurring event. The long agitation had shattered in pieces the old political parties of the country. Split asunder in their Convention at Charleston, the Democrats proposed two candidates to the people—Stephen A. Douglas, of Illinois, and John C. Breckinridge, of Kentucky. Disintegration had also invaded the old Whig Party. The Union wing of the Whig Party named John Bell, of Tennessee, for President. The Republican Party was increased by accessions from both the Whig and Democratic Parties, and announced the name of Abraham Lincoln as their chosen candidate. The county of Conecuh shared in the intense excitement that prevailed throughout the whole country. It was convulsed by the canvass. Little else was done this year, than discuss politics. Vast crowds would daily assemble at the places of popular resort, to canvass the questions at issue. Stump speaking was a daily occurrence. Men were swayed more by passion than by calm judgment. The storms of war were gathering thick and fast. The period of conflict had been reached.

The following is a list of county officers who served during the period embraced in the foregoing chapter:

JUDGES OF PROBATE.

1856—A. D. Cary.

SHERIFFS.

1857—A. B. Kennedy.
1860—Isaac D. Johnson.

CIRCUIT CLERKS.

1856—Mark B. Travis.

SENATORS.

1857—Daniel H. Horn.

REPRESENTATIVES.

1857—John D. Cary.
1859—John D. Cary.

CHAPTER XX.

Chapter of Biography—E. W. Martin—Rev. George Lee—Hezekiah Donald—Churchill Jones, etc.

EDMUND W. MARTIN.

This distinguished son of Conecuh was born near the city of Montgomery, on December 15th, 1821. He received his mental training at West Point. Through the influence of Senator Dixon H. Lewis, an ardent friend and relative of Mr. Martin, a cadetship was secured for him at the National Military Academy. Returning to his home from West Point, Mr. Martin's gifts led him into the forum, rather than the field. Having taken a course in law, he was admitted to practice, and commenced his career, as a lawyer, at Hayneville, about the year 1843. When the conflict with Mexico began, in 1846, Mr. Martin raised a gallant company in the county of his adoption, known as the "Lowndes County Volunteers," was made their captain, and went immediately to Mobile to offer their services to the government. Here they were received and mustered into the service of the government, but lack of transportation prevented their being transferred to the scene of action, and the war closed without their being able to participate. In 1849 Mr. Martin removed to Sparta, where he began a career which enabled him to make quite a reputation for himself as a practitioner of law. He was regarded by his brethren at the bar, as a close, calm reasoner, dignified, and keenly conscientious with regard to all questions of ethics. He was one of the readiest of speakers. A subject was quickly grasped by him, and even while the thought was warm, fresh from its new creation, he was giving it expression in elegant diction. During the war Mr. Martin raised a company of volunteers, of which he was made captain. Subsequently he became the major of the regiment to which his company was attached. During the battle at Dalton, Georgia, on the 24th and 25th of February, 1864, Major Martin was wounded by the fragment of a shell. In his command he was admired for the wonderful combination of kindness with firmness, in the exercise of discipline. At one time one of the men under his command became somewhat refractory, and it became necessary for him to give him some peremptory orders, which, with relutance, the soldier proceeded to obey, but with a protest in a low, under tone of voice, but sufficiently loud for every one to hear him say, "Well, never mind, every dog has his day." To which Major Martin replied, "That may be, if there are not more dogs than days." In politics, Major Martin was a life-long Democrat. In 1872 he was elected to the State Senate, from the district composed of Butler and Conecuh counties, but upon a contest, his opponent, Miller, was seated, not because he had received a majority of the popular vote, but because the Republican Party was dominant in the

Senate. In 1874, however, when the Democrats again attained the ascendency, Miller was legally ejected, and Senator Martin re-seated. The *Montgomery Advertiser*, in referring to his restoration to his seat in the Senate Chamber, said of him: "He is an able and watchful Senator, and possesses to the fullest extent, the confidence and esteem of his associates." He was the leading candidate for Lieutenant Governor in the Convention of 1874, and came within a fraction of a two-thirds vote upon the nomination. Also, in 1878, he was conspicuous as a candidate for Congress, and came within one vote of the nomination. On the 22nd of October, 1878, he died at his home, at Evergreen.

REV. GEORGE LEE

was a Baptist minister of some local distinction, and a member of one of the best families that ever resided in Conecuh. He was the seventh son of Justice Joel Lee, and brother to Revs. Hanson Lee, whose sketch has already been given, and David Lee, now of Lowndes county. George Lassiter Lee was born near Burnt Corn, on November 9th, 1819. When he was a lad of fifteen or sixteen, he became a Christian, and was baptized by Elder Alexander Travis. From the date of his conversion he had a disposition to attempt to preach, but great constitutional diffidence restrained him from the assumption of the sacred office for ten or twelve years. Yielding at length to those inward impressions, he became quite an effective minister of the gospel. During his early years he had received a thorough English training. Besides being a preacher of marked ability, he was a terse, vigorous writer. During his ministerial career, he served the Bethlehem Association, on different occasions, in the capacity of Clerk and Moderator. He was the Moderator of the body the year before his death. About 1871 or 1872, he died in the same section in which he had been reared. Mr. Lee was honored for his piety by all who knew him.

HEZEKIAH DONALD

was a native of Conecuh. He was a man totally unpretentious, and yet one of the most useful of men during his career. Such was his extreme modesty, that no emphasis was ever given by himself to the liberal benefactions which came from his hand. He found special delight in contributing to a cause, the object of which was the increased happiness or usefulness of his fellows. Diligent in the administration of his private affairs, he was prosperous. During the last few years of his life he was prominent as a successful planter. Mr. Donald died at his home, near Bellville, in 1861, much lamented by all who knew him.

CHURCHILL JONES.

The birth-place of Mr. Jones was Virginia. But little is known of his early career. He emigrated to Conecuh when a young man, and began teaching at Gravella. He soon found a charm in the agitated politics of the county, and ardently espoused the cause of the Whig Party. As the standard-bearer of that party he was sent to the Legislature for several consecutive sessions. He was regarded as possessing uncommon shrewdness in business, and within a few years after he came to the county he was the possessor of no mean wealth. His name is inseparable from the litigations which characterized the history of the county during his residence within it. He is remembered, to-day, as a most uncompromising litigator. In manners, Mr. Jones was affable and communicative. Several years before his death he removed to Texas.

JOHN W. ETHRIDGE.

The subject of this sketch came to Conecuh with his father's family when he was quite a small boy. He was born in North Carolina in 1810, and eight years later was residing near Brooklyn. Mr. Ethridge has led a quiet, unostentatious life. At different times he has been summoned from the solitude of home life, and by the popular vote elevated to positions of trust.

In 1870, he was regarded the most available man in Conecuh to defeat the notorious William P. Miller for the Legislature. In this his supporters were not disappointed. His unquestioned integrity, and sober, conservative spirit, secured to the party of the Democracy a majority, and he became the Representative of the county in the lower house during the sessions of 1870 and 1872.

Other positions have been held by him with credit

to himself and honor to his county. Though the frosts of three-score-and-ten winters have gathered upon his locks, he is, to-day, as elastic in his tread as a youth. Of him it may be almost as truly said as of the olden lawgiver: "His eye is not dim, nor is his natural force abated."

SHERMAN G. FORBES.

Many years ago there came to New England from Scotland two brothers whose names were Abisha and Squire Forbes. One of these settled in Salisbury, and the other in Canton, Connecticut. The latter of these, according to the history of that section, was the first smelter of iron in the United States. Abisha was the grandfather of Sherman G. and Dr. Solomon S. Forbes.

Sherman G. Forbes, familiarly known in all sections of the county as "Squire Forbes," was born in Canton, Connecticut, in the year 1813. His father was a native of the same section. Mr. Forbes removed to Alabama when he was quite a young man, and located at Sparta. Here he found employment as a clerk in the mercantile establishment of Robinson & Cary. He afterwards served Mr. Cary as clerk in the Land Office. Subsequent to this he was postmaster at Sparta, by appointment; and was also elected justice of the peace, which office he continued to hold for more than thirty years. He was, at length, elected to the position of tax assessor of the county, where he displayed such rare efficiency that he was re-elected for several successive terms. About the year 1845-'46, he was elected Clerk of the Circuit Court. In 1849, he engaged in a political contest with A. D. Cary for the Probate Judgeship. He was defeated by only thirty votes, and by a man of the most decided strength in the county. The close approximation to success in this election manifested the estimate which was placed upon his worth by the good people of Conecuh. Upon the resignation of Stephen C. Richardson as sheriff of Conecuh county, the office was tendered Mr. Forbes by the Governor of Alabama, but this offer he declined. At the close of the late war, he was appointed Revenue Assessor for the United States District, and none could have performed the duties pertaining to this office with greater efficiency. Mr. Forbes was a gentleman of even temperament, of much native dignity, and of superior qualifications for business. His memory was proverbially exact. The different stations held by himself during his life, had led him largely into the investigation of the legal science, and within a given compass of law no opinion could exceed his in exactness. He was freely resorted to for legal advice, which was gratuitously given. Politically, Mr. Forbes was a Democrat. He was emphatically a Union Democrat, both before and after the war. In March, 1876, he suffered from a paralytic stroke, from which he never recovered. After a sickness of seventeen days his spirit passed from earth into the boundless Beyond. The verdict of Judge Cary upon the reception of the news of his death, was that of every one who knew him with any degree of intimacy: "Conecuh county has lost one of its best citizens. He was the most correct business man I ever knew!"

DR. SOLOMON S. FORBES,

brother to Sherman G. Forbes, beheld the light, first, in 1827, in the town of Canton, Connecticut. He emigrated southward and reached Sparta in 1852, where he engaged in teaching a school. This he discontinued, however, after six months, and addressed himself to the study of medicine, under the tutorship of Dr. John Anderson. In 1854 he attended medical lectures in Albany, New York, at the Union Medical College. Here he graduated three months before the expiration of his term of study, received his diploma, and started westward. He opened an office at Sauk Rapids, in the Minnesota Territory, eighty miles above St. Paul. He continued his practice in this region for eight months, until the arctic breath of winter brought with it a vivid reminder of the bland climate and fervid skies of the far South, and without delay he left the hyperborean region of Northern Minnesota and returned to Alabama. Coming again to Conecuh, he located at Bellville, in 1856, and continued the practice of his chosen profession until 1872. During this interval he was President of the Board of Examination for the county, Vice-President of the County Medical Association, and 2nd Recording Secretary of the Medical Association of Alabama. During the year 1872 he removed to Milton, Florida, where he continues the practice of medicine. The citizens of Milton have honored him for three successive terms with the mayoralty, and upon his election the third time, it was his humorous boast that he had beaten General Grant for "the third term." Dr. Forbes is a gentleman of cultivated taste and of polished manners. A vein of genuine humor pervades his nature, which, coupled with his accomplishments, makes him quite companionable in the social circle.

MARK BUTLER TRAVIS.

Few men have left a more illustrious record to the future generations of Conecuh, than Mark Butler Travis. His life was one of chivalrous heroism and of devotion to his country. He was born in the neighborhood of Old Town, on May 18th, 1827. At quite an early age he evinced remarkable aptness in the acquisition of knowledge, while attending the schools of the neighborhood. Having pursued a course of medical study under the supervision of Dr. John Watkins, he left his home, when a stripling of only seventeen, to attend medical lectures in a distant State. But Mars was a more attractive personage to his chivalrous mind than Æsculapius, and while *en route* to college, he met the famous Palmetto Regiment, of South Carolina, on their way to join General Scott, in Mexico, and the blood of our young hero grew so warm within him, that he determined to enlist in the regiment and to go with them to Mexico. This he did, and shared with them the glories of Contreras and Cherubusco. In the latter named battle, he received a wound in the head, and was thereby prevented from being with his regiment when they entered the Mexican Capital. Recovering from his wound, he rejoined his comrades and served with patriotic efficiency throughout the remainder of the struggle. Returning to his home, he was honored by his fellow citizens with the office of Colonel of Militia, and was afterwards made General of Militia, over Col. Brock Henderson, of Butler. The people of Conecuh showed him deserved consideration by elevating him to the office of Clerk of the Circuit Court, which he held for four consecutive terms. He was universally known as an ardent Democrat, and yet such was his personal popularity, that serious inroads were invariably made by him into the ranks of the opposite party, and hence his unbroken political success. When again the clash of conflict summoned the men of the South to arms, General Travis was among the first to respond. He enlisted in the Conecuh Guards—the first company that left the county. He was made the 2nd lieutenant of this company, and went with it to Virginia. The following anecdote is related of him, as connected with the battle of Bull Run. At the time of the fall of the gallant Colonel Jones, the Fourth Alabama Regiment, to which the Conecuh Guards belonged, seemed threatened with utter extermination by the peculiarity of its surroundings. Becoming cognizant of this fearful fact, a panic seemed inevitable, and brave men began to turn their feet and faces toward the rear. Seeing the perilous situation, Lieutenant Travis endeavored to stay the flight of the regiment, and stood before the retreating columns with brandished sword, begging them not to fly. He was suddenly confronted by a burly Teuton, whose glaring eyes, open mouth and thin nostrils showed that he was the victim of a stupendous fright, and as he witnessed the efforts of Travis to check the flying columns, he blurted out: "O, mine friendt, my life is too schweet!" Lieutenant Travis, seeing that all efforts to arrest the flight were useless, himself joined in and sought a more secure position. He was sadly encumbered by a pair of heavy horse-skin boots, which provoked Dr. Taliaferro to say to him as he ran past: "Lieutenant, you had better look out, or Barnum will have those boots in his Museum before night!" The subject of this sketch died of pneumonia, at his home, in 1864. There were combined in his character many elements of true nobility.

JOHN DUDLEY CARY.

Conspicuous among the worthies of Conecuh county is he whose name is placed at the head of this sketch. He was brought to Conecuh, by his parents, when quite an infant, having been born in Sumter District, South Carolina, on the 20th of January, 1820. Having been reared by a father whose uprightness was proverbial in the county, Mr. Cary became an elegant gentleman, and one eminently fitted to the positions which he was summoned to occupy during his life. His first attainment to distinction was in 1841, when he had barely reached maturity. During this year he was elected county clerk, and in 1845 was re-elected to the same position. But for his personal popularity, he would have sustained defeat in the second contest, as he had to encounter the serious difficulties of leading a party whose voting power was in the minority, and of confronting a candidate who himself enjoyed the confidence of the people—William M. Bradley. The second victory of Mr. Cary was exceedingly creditable to him, as he led his opponent, in the face of the barriers already alluded to, with a majority of sixty-eight. In 1857 he was sent by the popular voice of the county to the Legislature. Having been renominated two years later, for the same office, he was again elected, defeating Hon. F. M. Walker. Like his father, he enjoyed the confidence of the masses, which was manifest whenever he presented himself before them for their suffrage. He removed to Florida in January, 1872, and died just a month later, leaving a wife and five children.

Chapter XXI.

The War Record of Conecuh—Intense Excitement—Conecuh Patriotism—Conecuh Guards, &c.

The election of Abraham Lincoln to the Presidency of the United States in 1860, was the signal for the clash of conflict. For successive decades the storm had been gathering, and the delay only rendered more terrific its fury when at length it did burst upon the country. Petty sectional issues had grown into giant proportions, and by their strength had drawn the North and South face to face, with demonstrations the most hostile. A review of these issues need not here be attempted, as they are familiar to all. We have only to do with the part borne in that period of carnage by the brave sons of Conecuh. Her people felt as deeply as did any, the force of the great questions which were moving the masses throughout the broad land of States. The withdrawal of Alabama from the Union, sent a tremor of patriotic thrill throughout the hosts of her brave men, and under the impulse of this power, they formed themselves into military organizations, and repaired at once to the scene of conflict.

Among the companies earliest enlisted for this approaching struggle, was that of the Conecuh Guards. They were organized at Sparta, April 1st, 1861, and on the 24th of the same month they left their homes for the seat of war in Virginia. Through the zealous efforts of some noble women, among whom were the Misses Stearns and Mathews, Mrs. Jay and Mrs. Dubose, a magnificent banner had been ordered for the gallant company, and reached Sparta just the day before their departure for Virginia. A large concourse had gathered at the Sparta depot to witness the formal presentation of the flag and to take affectionate leave of friends and loved ones. Master Henry Stearns held the banner during its presentation, and on either side of him stood three young ladies, dressed so as to represent the States that had withdrawn from the Union. Miss Irene Stearns represented South Carolina; Miss Kate Autrey, Georgia; Miss L. Henderson, Florida; Miss Mathews, Alabama; Miss C. Cary, Mississippi; Miss S. Crosby, Louisiana. This group, having been confronted by the company, drawn up in order, Miss Mathews proceeded to deliver the following

ADDRESS.

Gentlemen of the Guards:—The clouds which have so long impended over us, have burst at last in the fury of war, the tocsin has sounded, your country has summoned you to arms, and nobly answering to her call, you have assembled here to bid adieu to old familiar scenes and faces, and to receive in return our parting words of encouragement and cheer. We admire your valor, we love your patriotism, we partake of your enthusiasm, and as a token of these feelings we have assembled to-day, to present to you this banner, consecrated by a thousand loving wishes—a thousand earnest prayers. The light of spring is on the Southern hills, a thousand flowers lend fragrance to the breeze, a thousand birds are warbling songs of love—the friends of your youth, the companions of your boyhood, are around you—all is peace, and beauty, and tranquility. But the gleam of sunlight upon gay uniforms and flashing steel, reminds me (of what I would fain forget) that from all these you must turn away—that you must exchange the quiet of these green old woods, in all their spring-tide beauty, for the turmoil of the camp; sweet bird songs and loving tones, for the musket's rattle and the cannon's roar; kindly smiles and familiar faces, for the whizzing ball and deadly bayonet. In these perils we may not participate—we may not share with you the battle's rage, nor partake of the hardships and privations of a military career—but we, too, have our mission. It is ours to give you words of sympathy and cheer, to animate you by our enthusiasm, to encourage you to deeds of noble daring. Our prayers shall attend you our smiles shall welcome your return, and should it be the fate of any here to fill a warrior's grave, his name shall be embalmed with our heartfelt tears and cherished forever in our inmost memories. As the Spartan women in the olden times sent forth their loved ones to the battle, bidding them never to return unless graced with the laurel wreaths of victory, so do we now bid you go forth, to return to us only when our native land is free. I profess to be endowed with no gift of prophecy, but I *feel*, I KNOW, that the South will be victorious in the approaching conflict. Already has the telegraph brought to us "great news from the Carolinas," and our ears welcomed the salutes which ushered in the victory. Already has one important stronghold yielded to our arms, and the Black Republican flag gone down dishonored, before the proud banner of the Confederate States. Naturally gallant and chivalrous, the sons of the South have plucked Fame's proudest laurels

"On many a field of strife made red
By bloody victory."

In the thickest of the fight has ever rang the Southern war-cry; going as gayly to the battle as to a *fete champetre*. No foe has ever yet withstood the rush of Southern steel, and in such a cause as we are now engaged, our armies MUST prove invincible. Battling on their own soil, in the holy cause of Freedom, in defence of their homes and loved ones, and in short, of all that is nearest and dearest to the hearts of men, they will know no such word as "fail," and Victory must be their handmaid. The war may be long, it may be bloody, but there can be but one result—the eagle of victory will finally perch upon the banner of our young Republic. Go, then, "where glory awaits you," and may this flag, which, in the name of the ladies of Conecuh county, I present to you to-day, float ever like the white plume of King Henry of Navarre, in the very front of battle. Then

> "Take thy banner, may it wave
> Ever o'er the free and brave ;
> Guard it 'till our homes are free,
> Guard it--God will prosper thee."

At the conclusion it was presented to Captain Bowles, and, in behalf of his company, he expressed his thanks for this expression of encouragement.

The company embarked on the following morning for Montgomery, receiving a number of accessions to its ranks at Evergreen.* The organization and departure of the Conecuh Guards, were speedily followed by the organization of other companies in the county, while others joined companies from the surrounding counties. Quite a number of the gallant boys of Conecuh entered the ranks of the Monroe Guards. The patriotism of no county was more profoundly stirred than was that of Conecuh. Not only did brave young men leave the comforts and clustering associations of palatial homes, and set their faces toward the uninviting camp and the perilous field; but brave mothers, wives and sisters, sought to inspire them with timely words and deeds of sacrifice. And great was the patriotic generosity manifested by very many of the oldest citizens, in supplying the families of absent soldiers with food. Draught after draught, was made upon the barns and smokehouses of men too old for service, by the families of those upon whose labors they had been dependent for the neces-

---

*A complete list, together with a succinct history of the company, will be found in the Appendix.

sities of life. And after the first year of the war, vast quantities of clothing were manufactured by hands unused to work, and sent to distant camps. Every spinning wheel and machine, every card and needle, was drawn from its hiding place, and made to render service to a struggling people. With the closing of our ports, came the effectual check upon the importation of foreign luxuries, conspicuous among which were tea and coffee. But nothing daunted, divers substitutes were laid under contribution, and vast were the quantities of parched bran, peanuts and potatoes, that were served up to take the place of departed teas and coffees. And it may not be amiss, in this connection, to refer to the extraordinary conduct of the slave population of Conecuh, during the stormy days of the war. Never were a people truer to a trust, than were they. Instances were by no means rare, where the father and husband of the white family, had left wife and children in the midst of a vast throng of slaves, upon whom they had to rely for protection. And they were a cardinal factor in the prosecution of the war, not only as producers of the necessary supplies for the army, but as bulwarks of protection around Southern homes. In their artlessness they shared largely in the patriotic sentiment that swayed the families of their masters, and ofttimes from their demonstrative worship, could be heard the prayer on behalf of absent masters.

INVASION OF CONECUH.

After the surrender of the Florida coast to the enemy, Conecuh was repeatedly threatened with an invasion from the south. Remnants of commands were stationed at Pollard, and at points below, which, no doubt, served largely to check the advance of the enemy from that quarter. Not until early in 1865 was an invasion experienced by the people of Conecuh. Colonel Spurlin, at the head of a regiment of cavalry, advanced from the direction of Milton, Florida, *via* Andalusia, and struck the railroad at Gravella. Here they proceeded to displace the rails in such way as to bring the next south-bound train into direct conflict with the high embankments, which here line the railroad on either side. Upon the arrival of the train it was easily captured, with all its passengers. Proceeding southward, toward Evergreen, along the line of road, these undisputed masters of the situation found much pleasure in firing upon defenceless citizens. They entered Evergreen without encountering the slightest resistance, and proceeded to despoil families of silver plate and jewelry, and to rob the surrounding plantations of mules and horses. Proceeding still southward, they burnt the depot building at Sparta depot, and the jail at Sparta. The lurid glare of these burning buildings, at night, struck terror into the hearts of defenceless men and women.

The people of Bellville, having learned of the capture of their sister village, Evergreen, a body of mounted citizens proceeded in that direction, for the purpose of reconnoitering. When they had come within three or four miles of Evergreen, they suddenly encountered a small squad of Spurlin's command, that had been sent forward upon the Bellville road to guard against any sudden demonstration on the part of the citizens, while the chief command was moving along the dirt road toward Sparta. This squad had dismounted near the Bradley Plantation, in a sudden curve of the road, to burn a wagon, which had just been captured, when the Bellville deputation rode suddenly upon them. The surprise was equally shared in by both parties, but evidences of precipitate flight having been first given by the reconnoitering Bellvillians, nothing was left the invaders but a hot pursuit. With a clattering pell-mell, the citizen soldiery, still clinging to their shot-guns, fled back toward home. All would have reached their homes in safety, but for a diseased horse, which was ridden by Willie McCreary. Unable to keep abreast of the others in the stampede, his animal continued to slacken in speed until he was finally overtaken at Hunter's creek. Here, Willie, then a lad of sixteen, fell into the hands of the enemy, and was sent at once to Ship Island, as a prisoner of war. The extreme northern portion of Conecuh suffered somewhat from the depredations of Wilson's raid during the following month.

The events just recorded, were but the prelude of a scene of chaotic confusion throughout the county. Unfortunately for its inhabitants, this disaster was introduced just at a season when every thing turned upon activity on the farm, and when entire cessation of labor would have been well nigh calamitous. Following in the wake of these local troubles, was the surrender of the armies of the Confederacy, and the sudden close of the war. With the crops just springing into luxuriant promise, the slaves were liberated, and in their exhilaration, they left their old homes in vast crowds, and thronged the Federal camps. Utter lawlessness everywhere prevailed. Demoralization was wide-spread and rampant. Gloom was depicted in every countenance as men gazed upon a scene of universal disaster. The Southern soldier, returning to his home, after years of privation, either maimed or poverty-stricken, if not both, was confronted by the wreck and ruin of war. But with a heroism, just as marked as that which they had evinced on the weary march, or upon the field of carnage, they addressed themselves to the work of repairing their shattered fortunes, and of providing for loved ones. Their heroism was not more conspicuous under the leadership of Lee, Jackson and Johnston, than it was in peacefully following their vocations after the tattered banner had been folded, and the cannon hushed in silence.

The following is a list of the county officers who served during this period:

JUDGES OF PROBATE.

1862—A. D. Cary.*
1864—John M. Henderson.†

SHERIFFS.

1863—William M. Strange.

CIRCUIT CLERKS.

1864—William A. Duke.

SENATORS.

1861—D. C. Davis.
1865—William A. Ashley.

REPRESENTATIVES.

1861—William A. Ashley.
1863—William Greene.
1865—F. M. Walker.

---

*Disqualified by age in 1863.
†Appointed by Governor Watts to fill the unexpired term.

Chapter XXII.

A Chapter of Biography—James A. Stallworth—William A. Ashley—
Rev. W. C. Morrow—J. M. Henderson, etc.

JAMES A. STALLWORTH

was the most distinguished of the sons of Conecuh. Highly gifted with brilliant parts, of pleasing address and commanding person, he combined all the elements requisite to success in the realm of politics. He was born near the village of Evergreen, on April 7th, 1822. He became an orphan quite early, his mother having died when he was but three years of age. When he was but fourteen, he was left entirely parentless by the death of his father. His scholastic training was merely academical. His career as a student was spent in the academy at Evergreen. But such was the readiness with which he could always command his resources, that every one was impressed with the idea that his mental training was of the highest order. So deeply impressed was the Hon. Frank Beck, of Wilcox, with his social ease and graceful mien, and his ability as an orator, that he asked him, while both were representatives together in the Legislature, "Stallworth, from what college did you graduate?" He expressed great surprise when he was told, "I never attended college." At quite an early age Mr. Stallworth gave promise of future ability.

His powers of oratory were quite marked when he was but a boy. At the early age of eighteen he was married to Miss Harriet E. Crosby, eldest daughter of John Crosby. His marriage was quite fortunate for his future success in life. Inheriting, to a large degree, the energy and executive ability of her father, Mrs. Stallworth contributed largely to the growing success of her husband. Soon after his marriage he began planting, which he pursued for several years, when he was called into public life by having been nominated upon the Democratic ticket for Representative to the Legislature. In Mr. Mortimer. Boulware, young Stallworth found a strong opponent. He was a gentleman of great personal popularity and wealth, and was connected with one of the wealthiest families in the county. Mr. Stallworth, who had scarcely passed his twenty-second year, awoke a sensation wherever he went in the county, so brilliant was his oratory, and so cordial was his address. Large accessions were drawn from the ranks of the Whig Party, and he was elected, first, to the Legislature in 1845. He was renominated by the Democrats in 1847, and was again elected by a largely increased majority over his Whig competitor, Judge H. F. Stearns. During his last term of service in the Legislature he entered upon the study of law, and after adequate preparation, was admitted to practice. By force of talent he rose rapidly as a lawyer, having entered at once upon a most lucrative practice. So distinguished had his ability at the bar become, that in 1850 he was elected to the solicitorship of the Second Judicial Circuit. In this new position he had to encounter the ripe experience of one of the ablest bars in the State; and yet so nobly did he acquit himself that he came to be recognized as one of the best prosecuting attorneys the State ever had. In 1855 he resigned his position as solicitor and accepted the nomination for Congress of the Democratic Party, against Col. Percy Walker, of Mobile—the candidate of the Know-Nothing Party. Though defeated in this contest, Colonel Stallworth added new lustre to his rapidly-rising star, as an able debater and eloquent exponent of the political issues of the period. In 1857 he was again honored with the nomination of his party, for Congress. The result of this contest was the election of Colonel Stallworth, by quite a handsome majority, over Col. John McKaskill, of Wilcox. Two years later still, he was renominated for Congress, and this time defeated Col. Fred Sheppard, of Mobile. Colonel Stallworth remained in Congress until the passage of the ordinance of secession by the Alabama Convention, when he, together with the remainder of the Alabama delegation, withdrew. Returning to his home, he contributed largely of his means to the cause of the young Confederacy. His declining health forbade his entrance into the army, but his sons were among the first to enlist, though quite young. Colonel Stallworth died at his home, in Evergreen, on the 31st of August, 1861. During the brief period of sixteen years, he had occupied several of the most prominent positions in life.

Harper's Weekly, of February 9th, 1861, has this to say with regard to the subject of our sketch: "James A. Stallworth, who represents the First, or Mobile District, in the House of Representatives, was born in Conecuh county, Alabama, on the 7th of April, 1822. After having received an academical education, he studied law, passed a high examination, and has since enjoyed a lucrative practice. He was twice elected District Attorney for the circuit in which he practices, and was a member of the Legislature from 1845 to 1848. After having been defeated by the Know-Nothings, he was in 1857 elected to Congress, where he is a universal favorite, ever ready with an anecdote or repartee, yet none the less determined in maintaining the rights of his native State." Colonel Stallworth was a man of the noblest natural impulses. Most princely in hospitality, he frequently drew around his family board many of his truest friends. It is a matter of deep regret that one of such vast usefulness, and possessed with so many elements of greatness, should have been swept into a premature grave. He passed away at the early age of thirty-nine years.

WILLIAM A. ASHLEY.

The reputation enjoyed by this prominent Conecuhian was far from being local. His sterling ability was recognized throughout the Commonwealth of Alabama. William Adam Ashley was a native of Conecuh county, having been born in 1822. After an academical training in the schools near his father's home, he entered the East Tennessee University, at Knoxville, from which institution he was graduated. After his return to his home he married Miss Amanda Thomas, a daughter of Major Thomas. His attention was first devoted to planting,—but one with such distinguished qualifications for public service could not be suffered to address himself solely to his private interests. He was summoned into public life first in 1849, when the Whig Party of Conecuh named him as the champion of its principles, and nominated him for the Legislature. His success was easily attained. So conspicuous was his usefulness in his new *role*, that he was returned during the following canvass in 1851. Two years later he was elected to the State Senate, in which capacity he served for four years. In 1861 he was again elected to the lower house from Conecuh. During this year, too, he was Presidential elector for Messrs. Davis and Stephens. In 1865 he was returned to the Senate for four years—which terminated his public career.

Mr. Ashley was a man of solid, rather than shining qualities. Cool, deliberate, of unerring judgment, and withal, highly scrupulous, no one was better fitted than himself to serve his people during the trying ordeals through which they were called to pass during much of his public career. He was emphatically a patriot. Although he supported the Bell and Everett ticket in the memorable canvass of 1860, and though he opposed secession in 1861, Mr. Ashley did not falter a moment in sustaining the cause of the South throughout the hard struggle. "His wealth and his personal services"—says Mr. Garrett, in his "Public Men of Alabama"—"were devoted to the public defence." During the war many a Confederate soldier, weary and footsore oftentimes, found a cordial welcome beneath the hospitable roof of Mr. Ashley. After the close of the war, and when the work of the infamous Reconstruction measures was commenced in the South, Mr. Ashley denounced it in unmeasured terms as being the essence of tyranny.

He died at his home on Hampden Ridge, February 12th, 1870, and was buried in the Thomas burial ground. Thus there passed away that honored son of Conecuh before he had reached the meridian of life. Simple justice demands that appropriate reference be made in this connection to his most estimable wife, who honored her distinguished husband, and aided greatly in his elevation in life. The liberal and refined hospitality for which he was so noted, was enhanced by the conspicuous part borne by herself in its dispensation.

REV. WILLIAM C. MORROW

was a native of Pulaski county, Tennessee, where he was born on June 6th, 1815. At an early age he removed to Alabama, where he spent the major part of his life. When he was quite young, he was received as a member into the Presbyterian Church, and under its auspices fitted for the ministry. He continued his connection with this denomination until 1841 or 1842, when his views upon certain cardinal principles underwent a complete change, and he at once joined a Baptist church. His first charge was the Old Flat Creek Church, at Turnbull, in Monroe county. Remarkably gifted as a speaker, and unusually skillful in debate, he at once took high rank in the Baptist ministry. On different occasions he became the champion of his cherished principles in the field of polemics, and was justly esteemed an ardent advocate of the peculiar tenets held by his denomination. Such was the ability displayed by himself on several occasions, in the delivery of sermons, that their publication was earnestly sought, and they found enduring form in pamphlet shape. Mr. Morrow's secular interests, together with his declining health in later years, withdrew him gradually from the pulpit; so that, for more than an entire decade, toward the close of his life, he had no pastoral charge. He died at his home in Evergreen, on October 16th, 1879, in the sixty-fifth year of his age.

JOHN M. HENDERSON.

Among the men of worth produced by Conecuh is John M. Henderson. His place of birth was Brooklyn, and the time October 14th, 1824. He was educated in the schools of his native county, and never enjoyed the advantages of a course of training in college. Notwithstanding this, his mental attainments were by no means of a limited character. His mind was well stored with useful information gleaned from different fields of thought. His *debut* into public life was when his father, David F. Henderson, became sheriff of Conecuh. The son—then just budding into manhood—served the father as an efficient deputy. Subsequent to this he entered the mercantile business at Sparta, in which he remained until 1860. During this period he was treasurer of the county for one or two terms. In 1860 he removed to Pensacola, Florida, where, with marked success, he was engaged for some time as a commission merchant. Pensacola having become a scene of exciting hostility after the commencement of the war in 1861, Mr. Henderson returned to Conecuh and built a handsome home near Castleberry, and was instrumental in the establishment of a depot at that point. The advancing demands of the armies of the Confederacy for increased strength, made an appeal to the patriotism of Mr. Henderson, and such that he could not resist. Together with General Martin, he raised a company of volunteers, of which Martin became captain, and himself 1st lieutenant. The company was connected with the Thirty-eighth Alabama Regiment. Mr. Henderson remained in active service about two years, when he was appointed by Governor Watts, Judge of Probate of Conecuh county, to succeed Judge Cary, who had resigned because of a constitutional provision forbidding the occupancy of the office beyond a specified age. The ability which he brought to this new station enabled him to meet its demands in such way as to win distinction to himself and to impart unusual satisfaction to his constituency. This position he continued to hold until the dawn of the Reconstruction period, when he was ejected against the popular vote of the county, and A. W. Jones was elevated to the office.

Retiring to his home at Castleberry, he remained here but a short while, when he removed to Brewton, and thence to Mill View, Florida—at both of which places he was engaged in the milling and timber business, with varied success and misfortune. He died at Mill View, of typhoid dysentery, on September 9th, 1872. His remains were transferred to Sparta, where they were interred in the old family burial ground.

Judge Henderson was a typical Southern gentleman. Of commanding person and dignified mien, he excited the profoundest respect in every circle which he entered. His whole course of life bore the stamp of true manliness. He was exceedingly scrupulous with regard to the slightest promise. Toward the close of his life he evinced unusual solicitude in regard to his children, precipitated, as their lives had been, into the midst of the wide-spread demoralization which followed in the wake of the war. His family are still residents of the county.

DR. MILTON AMOS,

who was one of the earliest residents of the county, and for many years one of her most distinguished physicians, was born in the State of Maryland, about the year 1781. At an early age he turned his thoughts to the study of medicine, and afterwards finished his course in Philadelphia. Removing to Jones county, Georgia, he was married to Miss Reese. In the year 1818 or 1819 he came, with his young bride, to the wild scenes of South Alabama. His first point of location was at Cotten's Bluff, about twenty miles below Brooklyn. Here he resided for only a year, when he removed to Brooklyn, which gave early promise of vast importance in the future. When he came to this place, which afterwards became the most conspicuous point in the county, he found but two families residing here—those of Mr. Edwin Robinson, a merchant, and Mr. Thompson, the owner of the ferry on Conecuh river. During the period of his residence here, he had an extensive practice—reaching to all portions of the county, and even beyond. In 1835 he changed his location to Bellville. Again, he removed to Milton, Florida, in 1850. The town of Milton derived its name from that of his own. Dr. Amos died in Escambia county, in 1875, at the advanced age of ninety-four years. He has left a record of honored usefulness.

DR. WILLIAM CUNNINGHAM.

This distinguished physician was born in Mecklenburg county, Virginia, on April 21st, 1809. His medical training was secured in Philadelphia, where he was graduated when quite a young man. Returning to his Virginian home, he determined to seek a sphere for the exercise of his talents in the far South. Hence he removed to Alabama, and located first at Montevallo, in Shelby county. Thence he removed to Arkansas, and purchased lands upon Red river. A brief sojourn here was altogether sufficient to satisfy any longings which he might have had for the much-talked-of West, and he again turned his face toward Alabama. Removing farther south than before, he founded a home in Monroe county—the one now occupied by Hon. W. T. Nettles, and but a short distance from the present site of Kempville. In 1842, he served Monroe county in the lower branch of the Legislature. About this time he suffered the saddest of misfortunes—the loss of his wife—when he removed a few miles south of Burnt Corn, and built a handsome residence, just within the limits of Conecuh. Here he continued to reside until his death.

With remarkable success Dr. Cunningham combined planting with the practice of medicine. He shared in the general "wreck and ruin" incident to the war. By thrift and skillful management he had become the possessor of a vast estate before the war. Dr. Cunningham was a polished gentleman of the Old Virginia School. He was exceedingly polite, and his urbanity was extended to all alike.* Highly gifted as a conversationalist, and broadly informed upon all current topics, he was quite companionable. His scope of reading, however, was not restricted to the current

---

*The author remembers the impression produced upon his childish mind by the gentle politeness of Dr. Cunningham.

literature of the period. His fondness for study led him into the investigation of all sciences, alike. He was one of those remarkable spirits, who was prepared to impart information in regard to almost every subject. By the sprightliness of his conversation he always shed a wholesome radiance into the chamber of sickness. To these superior qualities of personal character was added that of exceeding great fondness for the fine arts. No one had a keener appreciation for excellent music, or works of art, than himself. Naturally hospitable, his pleasant home was the frequent resort of congenial associates. He contributed with unstinted hand to the war waged for Southern Independence. Besides contributing three sons to the armies of the Confederacy, he sustained the families of other men, who were absent upon "the tented field." Dr. Cunningham died at his home, on August 26th, 1867.

Chapter XXIII.

Dark Sway of Reconstructionism—Social Chaos—Demoralization—Local Troubles—Sovereignty of the Bayonet—The Negro as a Politician—How the New Order of Things Affected Southern Society—Heroism Displayed, &c.

Nothing equalled the wild chaos which prevailed in the South, just subsequent to the close of the war. The disorder introduced by invading armies, the derangement of the system of labor by the sudden emancipation of the slaves, the crash experienced by the heavy loss sustained by their former owners, the shock of disappointment at the failure of Southern arms—all these produced a universal gloom among the whites of the South. Exhilarated by the consciousness that he was no longer under the restraint of a master, the negro unceremoniously threw aside the implements of labor, and met his fellows where they were wont to gather, from day to day, in the rural village, at the depots, in the towns and crowded cities. All industry was suddenly paralyzed. There was a painful consciousness in the minds of the most reflective that no shield of legal defence existed, and that for once, society was launched upon a wild and stormy sea of disorder. Prompted by the innate principle of self-defence, every man resolved to protect, as far as possible, his own interests against the invasion of lawlessness. Hence it was to be expected that there would be occasional outbreaks of disorder. Robbery was by no means a rare occurrence, and here and there a murder was committed, while differences between the two races were frequently arising. Nothing of a serious nature arose in Conecuh. After the establishment, by the government, of military districts, troops were quartered at several points in the county, but here, as elsewhere, they were productive of more disorder than quiet. Every local camp became a kind of confessional, to which the negro would, for the most part, resort, not to confess his own sins, but to make confession of the sins of his white neighbor, and perhaps former owner, especially if these sins had the slightest relation to himself. Hence squads of cavalrymen were traversing the country districts, hunting up the perpetrators of reported misdemeanors, and great was the annoyance to which the people were subjected by these petty commanders of local posts. The feeling of demoralization, which came immediately upon the heels of the war, was gradually displaced by that of desperation, as the people witnessed the removal, by military orders, of the entire official incumbency of the civil positions, and their places filled by military appointees. Legally enfranchised, the blacks swarmed around the ballot-boxes at the first opportunity, and seemed greatly to relish the privilege of citizenship, though they were totally ignorant of the consequence of voting. Conflicting elements would soon have been tranquilized, and serene peace would again have smiled upon the desolate fields of the South, and would have kindled new hopes in the bosoms of her impoverished people, had not a horde of unprincipled politicians swarmed into the States, and fanned into intenser heat the hostility between the races. These, unfortunately, found fellow-helpers among the whites of the South, who, stimulated by no higher motive than self-aggrandizement, sought to widen the chasm between the races, in order to command the negro vote, and secure to themselves the spoils of office. Among those who contributed to this race agitation in Conecuh were William P. Miller and Rev. A. W. Jones.

In the midst of this wide-spread anarchy, created by the war and its disastrous results, it is wonderful that there was evinced such elasticity on the part of Southern society. A revolution could not have been more sudden or complete, than that into which the society of the South was precipitated; and yet the ease with which it was speedily adjusted to the existing order of things, was indeed marvelous. Men had risen from the most straitened circumstances into easy competency, and with a contentment at once natural and legitimate, were quietly resting from their early toils; and yet, when the crash of disaster came, they had to resume the hard labor of other days, in order to provide the actual necessities of life. Women, unused to domestic drudgery, and the thousand cares of which they had been relieved by competent servants, had to face the dire inevitable, and grapple with the duties to which a disastrous war had subjected them. But with the energy and elasticity for which the Anglo-Saxon race is so famous, these heroic men and women bravely met these trying odds, and distinguished themselves as signally as did their soldier boys upon the bloody field. Year by year, the South emerged from the wreck of the dark and bloody past, her people came more and more to take a calm and dispassionate view of "the situation," the lines of race prejudice were growing gradually dimmer, a spirit of industry began to awaken the sluggish energies of the people, and a wholesome change was being manifestly wrought in all directions.

The one event of marked interest in Conecuh, during the year 1866, was the removal of the seat of justice from Sparta to Evergreen. Two principal causes contributed to this removal. The first was the total destruction of the court house at Sparta, with all the county records, and the second was the growing importance of Evergreen, and its easy accessibility from all portions of the county. Two years later, Conecuh lost a portion of her southern territory by the formation of Escambia county. This county was established by an act approved December 10th, 1868. It was carved from Conecuh and Baldwin counties. It has not been allowed separate representation in the General Assembly, until the last few years.

List of county officers from 1865 to 1870:

JUDGES OF PROBATE.

1868—John M. Henderson.*
1868—A. W. Jones.

SHERIFFS.

1867—James Fortner.

CIRCUIT CLERKS.

1868— ——— Greenslate.†

REPRESENTATIVES.

1868—J. Yates.
1870—J. W. Ethridge.

---

*Removed by military force and succeeded by A. W. Jones.
† Of Illinois—appointed by the military authorities.

Chapter XXIV.

"Peep o' Day"—Darkness Clearing Away—Advancement of Order—Returning Signs of Prosperity—The People Becoming Themselves Again—A Glance at Current Events up to the Present.

The period about which I now write, was anticipated in the closing remarks of the last chapter. Several years elapsed before the people of Conecuh could withdraw sufficiently far from the reign of disorder to address themselves to the re-establishment of their institutions, and the resuscitation of their shattered fortunes. But a steady growing resolution was possessing the people, and gradually the signs of returning prosperity began to show themselves in every quarter. Of course this growing change was largely due to the revolution in politics. The combined powers of ignorance and selfishness were gradually giving way before the strong assertion of intelligence and public-spiritedness. Instead of being represented by men who were hostile to the public interest, the people were eventually able to send representatives of their choice. The wholesome legislation so sadly needed by the masses in their depressed condition, was eventually secured, and impartial officers elected to execute it.

The colored people, having realized the extent of the boon of liberation, and the relation which bound them to the whites, resumed, with commendable spirit, their former habits of industry in the field, the shop, the home, and thus contributed, in no small degree, to the prosperity which all, in common, now enjoy. Few have been the events that have disturbed the increasing growth of harmony in Conecuh, within the last few years.

In the summer of 1877 a painful event occurred in the quiet town of Evergreen, and one, the circumstances of which rendered it more painful, because of the parties connected therewith. Sheriff B. M. Burns, of Monroe county, while on official business in Conecuh, was engaged in a game of billiards with William Ashley, son of the late Senator Ashley, when a disagreement arose between them, and Mr. Ashley was shot and killed by Sheriff Burns. Intense excitement was created in both counties by the sad and unexpected tragedy, because of the prominence both of the slayer and the slain. After two years, Mr. Burns was tried at Evergreen and sentenced to hard labor for the county for a limited term of months.

To recount the events which have transpired from year to year, would be to tell the deeds of a determined people to make their section fairer, better and more inviting, than during any period of the past. Of the material elements with which they have to deal, I have occasion to write more at length in a subsequent chapter.

The following list contains the officers of the county from 1870 up to the present time:

JUDGES OF PROBATE.

1874—F. M. Walker.
1880—F. M. Walker.*
1880—Perry C. Walker.

SHERIFFS.

1869—James Fortner.‖
1874—John Angle.
1877—Robert J. McCreary.
1880—John Angle.

CIRCUIT CLERKS.

1874—George Christian.
1880—William Beard.

SENATORS.

1870—William Miller, Jr.
1874—William Miller, Jr.†
1874—E. W. Martin,‡
1877—J. H. Dunklin.§

---

* Resigned and was succeeded, by gubernatorial appointment, by his son, P. C. Walker.

‖ Retained in office, under the Reconstruction Acts, until 1874.

† Successful contestant of the seat with Gen. E. W. Martin, before the tribunal of a Republican Legislature.

‡ Seat given him upon the decision of the Democratic Legislature, that he was the year before fraudulently ejected.

§ Died before the expiration of his term.

1878—David Buell. ‖
1880—G. R. Farnham.

REPRESENTATIVES.

1872—N. Stallworth.
1874—N. Stallworth.
1876—A. J. Robinson.
1878—Eli Clarke.
1880—A. J. Robinson.

‖ Elected to fill unexpired term.

Chapter XXV.

Present Representative Men of Conecuh—Rev. Andrew Jay—Dr. J. L. Shaw, etc.

Approaching, as we are, the conclusion of our county history, so thrilling in historic event, and so conspicuous in the biography of prominent spirits, it has been thought proper to devote attention to those who are at present recognized as the representative men of Conecuh. Prominent among these is

REV. ANDREW JAY,

who is a native of the county, and has shared largely in its fortunes and its reverses. He was born within three miles of his present home, at Jayvilla, on February 16th, 1820. His father was one of the earliest emigrants to the county, and upon his removal hither was quite poor. But he was not lacking in those qualities of industry and economy, which invariably find expression in accumulation. His father surrounded himself and family with a competency of life's necessities. His son was early taught the habits of industry, and has led quite an active life. His mental acquirements were secured within the narrow compass presented by the school facilities of his boyhood days. When he had attained manhood the academy was established at Evergreen, and for three successive sessions, he studied there with vast advantage to himself. After his marriage to Miss Ashley—daughter of Capt. Wilson Ashley—he devoted his attention to planting. At different periods of his life he has been elevated to positions of trust and distinction. During the period when considerable attention was bestowed upon the organization of an efficient militia, Mr. Jay was selected as the major of a battalion. He was successively commissioner of roads and revenue, tax assessor and Representative to the General Assembly. For two consecutive terms he served Conecuh in the Legislature. Mr. Garrett, in his "Reminiscences of Public Men of Alabama," pays him a deserved compliment when he speaks of his ability as a legislator, and the marked attention bestowed by himself upon the interests with which his position was invested. Up to the period of the formal emancipation of the slaves, Mr. Jay had gathered about him a respectable fortune. And during the period of his prosperity, his liberality was proverbial. Whatever enterprise was inaugurated for the public weal, found a generous response at the hands of Mr. Jay. No one advocated with more profound earnestness the establishment of the railroad through Conecuh, than did he. He was one of the most liberal contributors to the enterprise. He gave largely to the endowment of Howard College, and the Southern Baptist Theological Seminary, at Louisville, Kentucky.

Aided by his noble wife, he found peculiar delight, during the war, in raising supplies of clothing and food for the Confederate soldiers, and shipping them to their distant encampments. Perhaps no one in the county has suffered more keenly the misfortunes entailed by the war, than Mr. Jay. Like many others, he was left by the cessation of hostilities, involved in financial embarrassments, arising mainly from security obligations. The burdens which he has borne would have crushed the spirit of many another man; but he has borne all with philosophic and Christian fortitude, and now the dawn of a brighter day is beginning to tinge the darkness of years. After retiring from the political arena, Mr. Jay was ordained to the Baptist ministry, and now his attention is divided between the farm and the pulpit. Throughout his life, his career has been such as should excite the profoundest admiration. He never swore an oath; was never engaged in a fight; was never intoxicated; never gambled in the least; was prompt in meeting all appointments made by himself. He is said never to have refused lodging to any one, upon application, except one time—then his family was quite sick, and the applicant quite drunk. His life has been largely devoted to the weal of his county.

DR. JOHN L. SHAW

is a native of North Carolina. He was born in Robinson county, in that State, on December 22nd, 1814. He was educated at Donaldson Academy, in Fayetteville, North Carolina. After engaging in teaching for a period of years, in his native State, he removed to

Alabama in 1841, and taught again at Prattville. Being desirous of fitting himself for the practice of medicine, he engaged to study with Dr. Kelly, of Coosa county. Subsequently he attended lectures at Louisville, Kentucky, returned to Alabama and practiced one year in Talladega, and in April, 1845, removed to Conecuh and located at Evergreen. After his marriage to Miss Permelia Crosby, he removed to Bellville, where, for quite a number of years, he engaged in an extensive and lucrative practice. In 1858 he removed to Pineville, Monroe county, thence to Evergreen in 1867, thence again to Pineville, in 1868, and finally to Bellville, in 1874. He was, perhaps, the first to suggest the preparation of the history of Conecuh. Dr. Shaw is appreciated for his disinterestedness in the public good, and for the uprightness of his daily life. Since his residence in the county, few men have been more active than himself, in the promotion of every public interest. Though quite advanced in years, he is still ardently devoted to the duties of his favorite profession.

YOUNG M. RABB.

The subject of this sketch was born in Old Town Beat, five miles east of Evergreen, on April 4th, 1826. His educational training was commensurate with the advantages enjoyed at that period. He was among the matriculates at the Evergreen Academy in 1840. Here he was fitted for a collegiate course, but was prevented taking such a course by the untimely death of a brother. By this event the management of his father's estate fell completely upon himself. But having naturally a sprightly mind, he continued to address himself to literary pursuits, as he had opportunity. In September, 1847, he connected himself with the Baptist Church at Evergreen, and shortly after became one of its deacons, which position he has held to the present. He was married, in 1848, to Miss Polly H. Stallworth, and at once turned his attention to planting. He was regarded a successful planter during the palmiest period of that pursuit in Conecuh. In 1856, we find him a citizen of Evergreen, whither he had removed for the education of his children. Here he formed a partnership with S. A. Barnett (now a citizen of Mobile), in a mercantile interest, which was conducted with success until the beginning of the late war. For many years Mr. Rabb was a member of the Commissioners' Court of the county, where he was exceedingly scrupulous in regard to the expenditure of the people's money. After the close of the war, he relinquished his farming interest, and embarked in a timber enterprise in Escambia county, Florida, as the partner of W. D. Mann. Here the failure of the contractors, under whose auspices the firm operated, involved it in serious embarrassment, thereby rendering Mr. Rabb unable to sustain that spirit of hospitality and benevolence for which he was characteristic during more prosperous periods. In 1880, Mr. Rabb offered himself to the people of Conecuh as a candidate for the Judgeship of the

Probate Court. He was, however, defeated by Judge Walker, a former incumbent of the office, and the regular nominee of the people. The many virtues of Mr. Rabb, his devotion to the public interest, and his intellectual qualifications, make him one of the representative men of Conecuh.

DR. A. J. ROBINSON.

This gentleman is a native Georgian. He was born in Fayette county, in that State, on January 16th, 1833. His parents were poor—but his father, by no means, humble in his influence. He was repeatedly elected to the State Legislature. For his public services he realized but little remuneration, and hence was unable to give his children the intellectual advantages which they might have otherwise enjoyed. The subject of our sketch was the eldest of the family of children, and upon him devolved the necessity of laboring upon the farm for the support of the younger children. He was an industrious laborer upon the farm until he was fully nineteen years of age, enjoying at brief intervals the advantages of country schools. But with his father absent as a public servant, and himself the first of a family of thirteen children, these opportunities for scholastic training were exceeding scant. At the age of nineteen, Dr. Robinson removed to McDonough, Georgia, where he attended a good school for six months. On the 17th of August of that year, he was married to Miss Josephine Moffett, of

Crawford, Georgia. She is the cousin of Col. J. S. Boynton, the President of the Georgia Senate.*

During the winter following his marriage, Dr. Robinson removed to Stewart county, Georgia, and began work upon a little farm, in connection with occasional intervals of school-teaching. In 1856 he sold his interest in Georgia, and removed to Covington county, in this State, settling upon Pigeon creek. In the midst of his varied reading he had acquired a peculiar fondness for the investigation of the science of medicine. Resolving to adopt the practice of medicine as a profession, he disposed of his place on Pigeon creek, and removed to Brooklyn, for the purpose of pursuing a more systematic course of study. Here, by stress of necessity, he was forced to divide his time between his studies and labors in the wagon shop of D. M. Dodson—his wife, meanwhile, assisting as teacher in the academy at Brooklyn. In 1857 and 1858 he attended lectures in Memphis, Tennessee. Here license to practice was granted him, and he returned to his home, and entered at once his chosen profession. In 1859 Dr. Robinson formed a partnership with Dr. John Scott; but after a year's connection with this gentleman, the copartnership was dissolved by the withdrawal of Dr. Scott. During the summer of 1859 Dr. Robinson attended another course of lectures at Atlanta, Georgia. Returning to his home, he found himself rapidly introduced into an

---

*In 1881.

extensive practice. For several years his practice in the portion of the county in which he resided was simply overwhelming. Declining health forced him gradually to retire. Since his retirement from the duties of a physician, he has been honored by the people of Conecuh during two different sessions with the position of Representative to the General Assembly. In this capacity he has proved to be quite useful, and has won for himself considerable distinction as a legislator. He served Conecuh during the last session of the General Assembly.

Dr. Robinson is a gentleman of many sterling qualities. His usefulness has been realized not only in direction of public affairs, but also in the sacred matters of the church. He is profoundly interested in the spiritual elevation of the masses. Possessing the highest sense of right, he is admirably fitted to become a prominent director in all matters relating to the public weal.

NICHOLAS STALLWORTH,

familiarly known as "Nick," is the third child of Hon. James A. Stallworth. He was born at Evergreen on the 9th of August, 1845, and hence is now but thirty-six years of age. He left school at the early age of fourteen, to accompany his father—then in declining health—to Washington. He spent the winters of 1859-'60-'61 in the National Metropolis. Returning with his father in 1861 to Conecuh, he at once joined the "Conecuh Guards," though he was a lad of only fifteen. His honored father accompanied him to Montgomery, and there meeting several of his quondam associates in the United States Congress—who were then members of the Confederate Congress—they proposed to secure for "Nick" the commission of lieutenant in the regular army. This was communicated to him by his father and friends; but the offer he politely refused, saying that he preferred a place in the ranks with the companions of his boyhood days. Upon the organization of the Fourth Alabama Regiment, he was found to be the youngest member in the entire command. He went with the Fourth Alabama Regiment to Virginia, and served in all the campaigns and battles in which it participated until the battle of Cold Harbor, where he was wounded and discharged. For some time prior to this he had been suffering from a bowel affection, and was in feeble health when he received the wound. Returning to his home, he found his mother stricken with grief by the double affliction of the loss of her husband and eldest son. The mother communicated to her son the dying request of his father, that if he should survive the bloody scenes of the war, he should go at once to the University of Alabama and complete his education. Regaining his health, "Nick" repaired to the University, and entered the Junior Class, in 1863. But his university course was cut short by sickness, and after an attendance of only eight months, he returned to his home. After the recuperation of his health, again he was offered a position on the staff of Gen. Samuel

Adams. But before the offer was responded to, General Adams was killed. He was also tendered a position on the staff of Gen. Thomas C. Hindman, but declined. Subsequently he accepted the Adjutancy of the Twenty-third Regiment of Alabama, then under the command of Maj. Nick Stallworth. Leaving at once for Virginia, he reached Petersburg; but the communication being cut between that place and Richmond, he was forced to turn his face homewards after several vain attempts to reach his command. The death of his brother-in-law, Captain Broughton, left him the oldest male member of the family, and he was forced to remain at home by the sad dependency of the family, combined with the shattered condition of his health. The war closing soon after this, he found himself ladened with unusual responsibilities for one so young. With no resources at command, he addressed himself with heroic spirit to whatever his hands found to do. After varied struggles with adverse circumstances, and hard labor with his own hands, for some time, he determined to address himself to the study of law. This he did with P. D. Page, Esq., and was soon admitted to practice.

In 1872, and again in 1874, he was chosen Representative from Conecuh to the Legislature. At the session of 1875–'76 he was elected Solicitor of the Eleventh Judicial Circuit. In this circuit he had to cope with many of the ablest legal spirits of the State, and yet his course was attended with remarkable success from the beginning. By the respectfulness of his deportment, and the urbanity of his disposition, he won the esteem of his legal brethren in all parts of the circuit; and by his efficiency and impartiality as a judicial officer, he secured almost universal popular esteem. He is justly regarded one of the most promising young men in the State.

COL. P. D. BOWLES.

Pinckney Downie Bowles is a native of South Carolina. His place of birth was Edgefield District. He received his educational training at the Citadel of Charleston, South Carolina, and at the University of Virginia. His collegiate course completed, he returned to his native State, and engaged in the study of law under Gen. Samuel McGowan.* He came to Alabama in April, 1859, and went into the office of Hon. James A. Stallworth, where he remained until the beginning of the war. In 1860 he was elected Colonel of the Twenty-eighth Regiment of Alabama Militia; and also 2nd lieutenant in the "Conecuh Guards," in the summer of 1860. In January, 1861, he went in that capacity with the company to Pensacola. When the company returned home, and upon its reorganization, he was chosen captain, and went with his gallant company to Virginia. Henceforth the war record of Colonel Bowles is inseparably connected with the illustrious career of the Fourth Alabama Infantry— "of which he was the brave and faithful commander" almost throughout the entire war. He led his regi-

---

*Now on the Supreme Bench of South Carolina.

ment into the majority of the fiercest battles fought on the soil of Virginia. The regiment belonged to the famous brigade commanded by General Bee, who was so conspicuous at the first battle of Manassas. It was in the battle of Seven Pines, Cold Harbor, Malvern Hill, Second Manassas, Boonsboro', Sharpsburg, Fredericksburg, and Suffolk. It joined in the invasion of Pennsylvania, and was engaged in the fierce conflict at Gettysburg. It went with Longstreet when he was sent to reinforce Bragg in North Georgia; it returned with him when he marched through East Tennessee, *via* Knoxville. Rejoining the Army of Northern Virginia, it was engaged in the battle of the Wilderness, and at Spottsylvania. In the operations of the Second Cold Harbor it was again engaged; and then lay for ten months behind the defences of Petersburg, sharing in the various movements and assaults connected with that eventful period. And finally, with ranks depleted by death and disability, it surrendered with the rest of the army at Appomattox Court House, with two hundred and two men.

During this long and bloody period, Colonel Bowles was ever found at the head of his regiment. I believe only one brief respite from service was given him— and that was on the occasion of an amorous mission to his adopted county in February, 1863, when he was married to Miss Stearns, daughter of the late Judge Stearns.

Though Colonel Bowles did not receive his commission as brigadier, he was placed in the command of five regiments, near the close of the war, and a full brigade staff ordered to report to him. When he returned to Conecuh, in 1865, he had but fifty cents in his pocket. Without delay, he opened an office at Sparta, and resumed the practice of law. The following year he was elected county solicitor for Conecuh, in which position he served for a long period, with efficiency.

Though having so eventful a record, Colonel Bowles is still comparatively a young man. He is now a resident of Evergreen, and is a successful practitioner of law.

GEORGE ROBERT FARNHAM.

This prominent young attorney was born near Bellville, on January 23rd, 1845. He was reared by his great-grandmother, Mrs. Nancy Savage, whose piety and usefulness were proverbially known for many years, throughout Conecuh. His course of instruction was cut short at the Bellville Academy, by enfeebled health, when he had reached the age of fifteen, and was recuperated by active work on the farm. When a youth of only sixteen, he enlisted in the Confederate army, having joined the "Monroe Guards," under Capt. Giles Goode. He went with his command to Pensacola, whence, after a brief service of three weeks, it was ordered to Virginia. Near the close of 1861 he was prostrated by a protracted attack of measles; he was discharged and returned to his home. The following year he resumed his studies at the

Bellville Academy, and in the fall of 1862 was entered as a cadet upon the matriculation roll of the University of Alabama. In the early part of 1865 he graduated in the regular course of that institution, with the exception of mathematics, and was pursuing the last studies in that branch when he retired. His course at the University was marked with distinction. He was appointed first a sergeant in the corps, then promoted to a second lieutenancy, afterwards to the adjutancy, and when he left the University he was senior 1st lieutenant. While at the University the corps of cadets did service, as soldiers, for three weeks in Mobile, and again at Jacksonville. In 1864, while going home upon a tour of vacation, about fifty or sixty of the cadets reached Montgomery, where they found the city in the midst of the most intense excitement, growing out of the threatening demonstrations of General Rousseau. Governor Watts ordered the cadets to remain in Montgomery and assist in its defence against Rousseau, who was then at Chehaw. Arms having been furnished them, a soldier of the regular army was appointed to the command, and they were permitted to elect their other officers. Mr. Farnham was at once chosen 1st lieutenant, and the buoyant cadets leaped upon the train and started at once for Chehaw. They were accompanied by some regulars, who happened to have been in Montgomery at the time, and also by some raw reserves. But for the military training and thorough efficiency of the cadets, the entire command would have been captured, and the city of Montgomery would have fallen. Subsequent to this, Mr. Farnham served as adjutant in the corps of cadets, near Spanish Fort. In the early part of 1865 he raised a cavalry company among the students of the University, which was designed to serve as the body-guard to General Buford, and the company left the University, to return to their homes to secure horses and equipments; but just at this juncture the State was overrun by the Federal troops, and before a thorough organization could be effected, the war closed. In 1866, Captain Farnham commenced the study of law in the office of General Martin, at Sparta, and in September, of the same year, was admitted to practice. The first year of his legal career was spent as a partner of General Martin, after which he practiced alone, until his late connection with M. S. Rabb, Esq. In 1868 he was elected a member of the Executive Committee of the Democratic Party of Conecuh, and in this capacity served without intermission, for ten years—the last four of which he was the chairman of the committee. In 1870 he was unanimously nominated for the county solicitorship, by the Democratic Party, but was defeated by the Radicals. In August, 1876, Captain Farnham, underwent the greatest of all changes—the renovation of his spiritual character. He became at once an active member of the Baptist Church at Evergreen, and finds peculiar delight in the work pertaining to the office of Sunday School Superintendent. In 1880 he was elected the President of the State Sunday School

Convention. During the same year he was nominated for the Senatorship of his district, and was overwhelmingly elected—having received the largest vote ever cast in the district, 5,435. He was sustained by both the Democratic and Republican Parties. During the approaching session he signalized his usefulness as a legislator, by securing the passage of a bill providing for the humane treatment of prisoners—the proper ventilation, heating of cells, and the proper supply of pure water for drinking purposes. He also secured an amendment to the section of the code relating to the regulation of the hire of convict laborers, so limiting the time as not to remand persons to slavery under the color of law. He earnestly strove to secure the passage of bills relative to reformation in the voting system of Alabama. In this he encountered strong opposition in the State Senate. His object was to secure an amendment to sections 274–276 of the code, relative to numbering and the size of ballots. By dilatory motions and parliamentary manœuvring, the action upon the bills was delayed. By resolute effort he forced a vote upon them toward the close of the session, and lacked only a few votes of securing the passage of the bill providing for the numbering of ballots. His speech upon the election law was published in the *Montgomery Advertiser*, and won alike the approbation of the press and the people. For one so gifted, so young, and energetic, and withal so virtuous in his life, there is a future of the most radiant promise.

Chapter XXVI.

Population—Principal Town—Climate—Soil—Stock Raising—Productions—Industrial Resources—Forests—Streams—Numerous Advantages, Social, Educational, Agricultural—Colored Population, &c.

According to the late census* Conecuh has a population of 12,606. The population would have been much greater had the county retained its original territorial limits. By the formation of Escambia county, in 1868, Conecuh lost much of her southern territory, which included several thousand of her population. Among her numerous villages, Evergreen, the county seat, is the largest. It is one of the thriftiest towns of Southern Alabama; is situated on the Mobile and Montgomery Railway, nearly mid-way between these two cities, and has a population of nearly 800 inhabitants. Its location, in one of the most productive regions in this section of the State, the elevated tone of its society, its educational and religious facilities, and its mineral springs, make it quite a desirable point.

Conecuh county lies in the southern part of Alabama, and is within the southern portion of the temperate zone. Its climate is such as to exempt it alike from the rigors of a Northern region, and the disease and debility of the tropics. The mean annual tem-

---
*1880.

perature is about 65 degrees. Within the limits of the county can be found every variety of soil, from the most productive to the most barren. From the centre of the county to its northern limits are to be found lands of great fertility, while in the southern portion the lands are for the most part, thin, but by no means valueless. In the earliest periods of the settlement of the county, the lands which lay along the streams had a deep alluvial soil, that had been enriched for ages by the steady influx of productive deposits. And when the forests were felled, and the implements of industry had begun to stir the soil, the yield from these lowlands was immense. The basin lands of Murder creek, Conecuh river, Bottle creek and the Sepulgas, furnished the most productive soil found in the county. Adjoining these regions, though elevated to uplands, are the red lands of the county, which are regarded the most unfailing and uniform in their yield, as well as being most resistful to the power of waste. In the lower portion of the county are the pine districts, made famous, in late years, by the vast quantity of timber furnished to foreign ports. Since the earliest settlement of the county, these regions have been held in high esteem as pasturage lands. The absence of undergrowth or shrubbery, gives unbounded freedom to the luxuriant grass that flourishes throughout this entire section. Though naturally thin, the soil is susceptible to a high degree of artificial cultivation, as there is usually found in this sandy region, a deep sub-soil of clay. These regions of sand and pine, though prevailing almost uninterruptedly in the lower half of Conecuh, are found in many portions of the county. These lands, almost without exception, are of level surface, thereby rendering quite easy the retention of fertilizers. And it is a subject of inquiry, if, with their subsoil of clay and their level surface, they are not destined to become the most unfailingly-productive lands in the county. It is a subject of regret that so many of the best lands of the county have been surrendered to the sway of "the tangled vine and riotous weed." Where once there waved the harvests of plenty, there are to be found, to-day, in many places, the thicket of briar and rustling sedge. Having undisputed sway, the early farmers would betake themselves to the invasion of uncleared forests, as soon as it became evident that their lands were being impaired by usage, and they would thus leave behind them broad acres of soil that needed but little careful attention to preserve their wonderful productive powers. These lands are only awaiting the hand of industry to become again the most yieldable in the county.

STOCK RAISING.

Conecuh is peculiarly adapted to the raising of cattle, sheep, hogs and goats. Her extensive areas of grassy lands, which are covered with a verdant and luxuriant herbage, almost the year round, and well-watered with perpetual streams, places Conecuh in the front rank of stock-producing counties. In addition to the growth of these tender grasses, there is that of the wild cane, which grows throughout all seasons along the streams, and is much relished by every variety of stock. Beef in considerable quantities, and of superior quality, has for a long time been furnished from these, and adjoining regions, to the markets of Pensacola and Mobile. The production of wool is beginning to excite considerable attention in the county, and the time is not distant when it will become a source of vast revenue to the county.

FORESTS.

The prevailing growth in the forests of Conecuh is that of the hickory, poplar, ash, beech and pine, all the varieties of oak, and the queenly magnolia. The uncleared districts of the county cover at least 75 per cent. of its surface. Along the streams, and upon the most fertile soil of the county, are found abounding the oak, the hickory, and beech—the annual yield of whose fruit fattens hundreds of hogs. And in the near future the hand of Art will be laid upon these useful timbers, and they will be made serviceable in the homes and trades of men. For many years past, the pine timbers of Conecuh have been a profitable commodity to dealers in lumber. Hewn into proper shapes, these timbers are floated in rafts down the principal streams to Pensacola, whence they are transported to the ship-building yards of different countries.

Through the enterprise of Messrs. Bellingrath and

Redwine, a turpentine manufactory has just been established at Castleberry. This article will no doubt become quite a commodity in the future commerce of the county.

PRODUCTIONS.

The productions of Conecuh are as varied as the soil upon which they are grown. The soil is peculiarly adapted to the growth of cotton, which is its all-prevailing staple. All the cereal crops, except wheat, are cultivated and yield in abundance. Improved systems are obtaining very generally throughout the county, and as a consequence, production is progressive.

Of staple farm products, corn, oats, rye, peas, rice, potatoes, peanuts, millet, sugar-cane, and cotton, are produced quite early.

Of fruits, the apple, pear, peach, fig, grape and melons, are the chief productions. Vast varieties of grapes are being introduced into different parts of Conecuh, and they never refuse to yield handsomely. The forests and abandoned fields abound in nuts, grapes, and berries, in large variety, which are furnished by Nature without cultivation. Because of the diversity of soil, the variety of productions, the favorableness of climate, and the easy accessibility to market, no field is more alluring to the immigrant than Conecuh. Vast regions of her land can be purchased at figures quite low. To the farmer, the horticulturist, the gardener, the shepherd, and the manufacturer, facilities are afforded for easy settlement and rapid accumulation.

GEOLOGICAL RESOURCES.

Within the county is found a great variety of useful stone. In different sections the lime rock abounds. Mica has been discovered within the last year in such quantities as to encourage the hope of future profit.

STREAMS.

Conecuh is penetrated in different directions by some of the noblest streams of South Alabama.

Along its eastern border runs the Conecuh river into which flows Sepulga and Bottle creeks, while farther in the interior is Murder creek—a stream of great width and depth—and the southern portion is watered by Burnt Corn creek and its numerous tributaries.

SOCIAL AND EDUCATIONAL ADVANTAGES.

The county of Conecuh will compare favorably with any other in the State, with respect to the tone of its society and the character of its institutions. The society is, for the most part, moral and refined. Schools and churches abound. Two academies of high grade are to be found—one at Evergreen and the other at Bellville—presided over respectively by Professors Tate and Newton.

THE COLORED POPULATION.

The colored people of the county are as intelligent, industrious and thrifty as any in the South. Since

220   HISTORY OF CONECUH.

their emancipation many have secured comfortable homes by energy and frugality. There is a number who are well-to-do—having amassed to themselves respectable property.

CLOSING REMARKS.

Together, dear reader, we have passed over the scenes enacted in the county of Conecuh from the time that the first white man faced its perilous wilds, to the present time. Through all the shifting scenes incident to human life, we have passed, in this rapid review. Together have we stood with the gray-haired sires of the long-ago, and gazed upon the sunlit hills and green valleys of Conecuh, ere the tread of civilization broke their slumbering echoes. We have seen the hardy settler leave his home in the distant States and confront the barriers and hazards of a long journey, and finally pitch his home in a region as yet unwrenched from the grasp of the wild savage. We have seen the heroism with which he addressed himself to the colossal task of subjecting the wild forces of nature to his control. We have watched the growth of civilization along successive decades, and have seen its struggles with frowning disadvantages. Through poverty and pinching distress, through smoke of battle and radiant prosperity, we have come up to the Present. And looking back from our present eminence-height, along the stretch of past years, we see the monuments of worth erected along the track of six and a half decades—

monuments reared by the energy and pluck of our fathers and grandfathers,—yea, we see a county reclaimed from its wilderness wilds and made to "rejoice, and blossom as the rose." The determination to snatch from oblivion the records of their heroism and success, and embody it in perpetual form, was alike honorable to sire and son. These brave men and women of the past, many of whom slumber beneath the sods of Conecuh, have bequeathed to the present and succeeding generations a rich legacy—a priceless bequest—in their deeds of nobleness; they "being dead, yet speaketh." Upon the generation of the present—the sons and grandsons of a noble ancestry—rests the duty of continuing the work of advancement commenced sixty-six years ago, when Conecuh was enfolded within her own virgin forests. Let them seek to preserve intact the institutions designed to ennoble the masses, and let them be as diligent in service to the generations to follow as were their ancestors to the generation of the present. So shall Conecuh continue her onward progress, and her people shall continue to be elevated in the scale of intellectual and moral excellence, "to the last recorded syllable of time."

THE END.

APPENDIX.
I.

CONSTITUTION OF THE CONECUH HISTORICAL SOCIETY.

PREAMBLE:

Whereas, the citizens of Conecuh county being desirous of reclaiming from the obscurity of the past, all the elements which will serve to make a correct history of the county, have agreed to constitute a Society for that purpose, to be governed by the following Constitution:

ARTICLE I.

Section 1. The name of this Society shall be "The Conecuh County Historical Society."

Sec. 2. The object of this Society shall be the accumulation and compilation, in enduring form, of the events which have marked the history of the county in the past, reaching back to its earliest period, and also of the men who have flourished in its annals, and indeed of every object and item which would serve to contribute, in anywise, to the interest of the history of a people.

Sec. 3. The officers of this Society shall be a President, two Vice-Presidents, a Recording Secretary and a Treasurer, who shall perform the duties usually connected with such offices.

Sec. 4. In addition to the above officers there shall be an Executive Committee of five, composed of four members to be chosen from different parts of the county, and the President of the Society, who shall be *ex officio* Chairman of the Committee. The duty of this committee shall be to appoint time and place of meetings, arrange programme of exercises, and do whatever else will be demanded for the success of each occasion.

Article II.

Section 1. This Society shall be composed of all who are or have been citizens of this county, who may desire to unite therewith. A list for the enrollment of names shall be kept in the office of the Judge of Probate, and a Recorder shall be appointed in each Beat, whose duty it shall be to secure the names of citizens, and forward weekly to the Judge of Probate at Evergreen.

Sec. 2. The members of this Society shall secure material from every possible source that would in anywise contribute to the history of the county, whether traditional, biographical, martial, agricultural, or otherwise.

Sec. 3. Material thus secured must be forwarded to the address of the Chairman of the Statistical Committee, at Evergreen.

Sec. 4. This Constitution may be amended by a majority vote at any regular meeting of the Society; provided, that notice of such proposed amendment be given at a previous meeting.

APPENDIX II.

CONECUH GUARDS.

COMPANY E, FOURTH ALABAMA REGIMENT.

Below is given a complete roll of this company, which was the first organized for the war in Conecuh.

It was permanently organized at Sparta, Alabama, on the 1st day of April, 1861; mustered at Sparta Depot, April 24th, 1861; received flag from the Ladies of the county; embarked on train with the following named commissioned, non-commissioned officers and privates; mustered into the Confederate States Army at Lynchburg, Virginia, May 7th, 1861; surrendered at Appomattox Court House, Virginia, April 9th, 1865:

Bowles, P. D., captain; promoted major, August 22, 1862; lieutenant colonel, September 30, 1862; colonel, October 3, 1862; brigadier commander C. S. A., April 3, 1865.

Lee, William, promoted captain from 1st lieutenant, August 22, 1862; wounded at Gaines' Farm, Virginia, 1862; killed at Gettysburg, Pennsylvania, July 3, 1863.

McInnis, Archibald D., promoted captain, from 1st lieutenant, July 3, 1863; retired from wounds received at first Manassas, July 1861, and at Gettysburg, Pennsylvania, July 3, 1863, and at Cold Harbor, Virginia, 1864; died in Mobile, Alabama, since the war.

Darby, James W., promoted captain, from 1st lieutenant, 1864; wounded at Gaines' Farm, 1862; resides in Butler county, Alabama.

Guice, John G., promoted 1st lieutenant, from 2nd lieutenant, August 22, 1862; wounded first battle Manassas, Virginia, July 21, 1861; wounded at Gaines' Farm, Virginia, July, 1862; wounded in two places second battle Manassas, August, 1862, lost leg; honorably discharged; resides in Conecuh county, Alabama.

APPENDIX.

Christian, Alfred, 1st lieutenant; wounded second battle Manassas, Virginia, August, 1862; died in Conecuh county, Alabama, since the war.

Travis, Mark B., 2nd lieutenant; honorably discharged, April 1, 1861; died at Sparta, Alabama, during the war.

Taliaferro, Charles T., 2nd lieutenant; resigned 1862; promoted to assistant surgeon 1862; promoted full surgeon Fourth Alabama Regiment, 1864; resides in Conecuh county, Alabama.

Stearns, John S., 2nd lieutenant; wounded at Knoxville, Tennessee, November, 1863; wounded at Wilderness, Virginia, May 6, 1864; died at his home in 1880.

Gatch, Louis, 1st sergeant; killed first battle Manassas, Virginia, July 21, 1861.

Green, William, 1st sergeant; honorably discharged 1863, on election to Alabama Legislature; resides in Washington county, Alabama.

Mosley, Andrew J., 1st sergeant; wounded first battle Manassas in head and arm; wounded at Gettysburg, Pennsylvania, July, 1863; wounded at Chickamauga, Georgia, September, 1863; wounded at Spotsylvania Court House, Virginia, May 9, 1864; resides in Falls county, Texas.

Downs, George, 2nd sergeant; killed at Chickamauga, Georgia, September, 1863.

Cotton, James, 4th sergeant; taken prisoner at Gettysburg, Pennsylvania; remained in prison to the end of the war; died in the State of Texas since the war.

Richey, Robert, 3rd sergeant; killed at Gettysburg, Pennsylvania, July, 1863.

Stinson, Jasper Newton, promoted to color sergeant Fourth Alabama Regiment, July, 1862; killed at the second battle Manassas, August, 1862.

Boulware, Gil R., promoted to color sergeant Fourth Alabama Regiment; wounded at Fredericksburg, Virginia, September, 1862; wounded in side and arm, and right arm amputated, at Chickamauga, Georgia, September, 1863; resides in Conecuh county, Alabama.

APPENDIX. 227

Spence, Ingram, sergeant; recruited November, 1861; wounded at Knoxville, Tennessee, September, 1863; resides in Conecuh county, Alabama.

Clark, William D., sergeant; recruited November, 1861; wounded at Gaines' Farm, July, 1862; wounded at Spotsylvania Court House, Virginia, May 10, 1864; resides in Conecuh county, Alabama.

Dunham, John Q., sergeant; wounded at Chickamauga, Georgia, September, 1863; died in Madison county, Florida, 1878.

Andrews, James M., sergeant; wounded first battle Manassas, Virginia; resides in Conecuh county, Alabama.

Floyd, Alfred H., 2nd sergeant; recruited November, 1861; wounded at Gettysburg, Pennsylvania, July, 1863; wounded (lost leg) at Wilderness, Virginia, May 6, 1864; honorably discharged; resides in Texas.

Stahl, Louis, 3rd sergeant; wounded and arm resected at Petersburg, Virginia, October, 1864; resides in Marlin, Texas.

Thomas, William, 1st corporal; killed first battle Manassas, Virginia, July 21, 1861.

Briley, Thomas, 1st corporal; killed at Chickamauga, Georgia, September, 1863

Richey, James, 1st corporal; killed at Knoxville, Tennessee, October, 1863.

Roach, Fred. G., 2nd corporal; killed at Petersburg, Virginia, April 1, 1865; last man ever killed in company E.

Crosby, William S., 1st corporal; resides in Conecuh county, Alabama.

Thomas, Joseph A., 4th corporal; wounded first battle Manassas, Virginia, July 21, 1861; wounded at Eltham's Landing, Virginia, April, 1862; wounded at Gaines' Farm, Virginia, 1862; wounded at Fredericksburg, Virginia, 1863; wounded at Gettysburg, Pennsylvania, 1863; resides in Conecuh county, Alabama.

Anderson, W. F., 2nd corporal; wounded at Fredericksburg, Virginia; died at Sparta, Alabama, since the war.

Robertson, James, 3rd corporal; wounded in three places at Sharpsburg, Maryland, September, 1862; wounded at Wilderness, Virginia, May 6, 1864; resides in Conecuh county, Alabama.

Anderson, George, recruited in fall 1861; killed battle Lookout Mountain, October, 1863.

Akerman, John, recruited January, 1865; wounded at Farmville, Virginia, on retreat from Petersburg; whereabouts unknown.

Alford, Artemus S., recruited January, 1865; resides in Texas.

Beard, Blake, wounded first battle Manassas, and discharged (honorably); resides in Conecuh county, Alabama.

Bonnett, J. B., wounded first battle Manassas; discharged, 1862, (honorably); resides in Conecuh county, Alabama.

Betts, Frank, returned home on sick furlough, and died in fall 1861.

Betts, Ed., discharged in summer 1861; rejoined some other command and was killed in East Tennessee.

Blakely, G. W., discharged in fall 1861; run over and killed by cars since the war.

Booker, W. B., wounded at Chickamauga and disabled for life; resides in Conecuh county, Alabama.

Baggett, Richard, recruited in fall 1861, and died from sickness, in hospital, in the winter of same year.

Brown, Julius, recruited in April, 1862; died from sickness, in the hospital at Charlottesville, Virginia, in the spring of 1862.

Brown, Robert, recruited in April, 1862; died in hospital at Richmond, Virginia, from sickness.

Brown, William, recruited November 1861; deserted May 1, 1863.

Burk, William, recruited November, 1861; died in Montgomery county, Alabama, since the war.

Carter, D. L., recruited November, 1861; wounded at Suffolk, Virginia; resides in Conecuh county, Alabama.

Cooper, M. A., wounded at battle Wilderness, May 6, 1864; resides in the State of Texas.

Chapman, Henry C., recruited March, 1864; wounded at battle Wilderness, May 6, 1864; placed on retired list; resides in Texas.

Curlee, F. M., recruited November, 1861; wounded at Gettysburg; whereabouts unknown.

Coleman, Henry C., died at Richmond, June, 1862.

Coleman, William, recruited November, 1861; killed at battle Gettysburg, July 3, 1863.

APPENDIX. 229

Cato, A. J., recruited November, 1861; discharged for disability; resides in Texas.

Downs, Jerre, killed at battle Gaines' Farm, July, 1862.

Daniels, J. W., recruited 1862; wounded at Fort Harrison, 1864; resides in Conecuh county.

Dyas, Thomas, taken prisoner at Knoxville, 1864; died in prison.

DuBose, James, killed at Chickamauga, September, 1863.

Dean, Thomas, recruited November, 1861; deserted to the enemy at Strawberry Plains, Tennessee, 1863.

Douglas, William, honorably discharged, July, 1862; residence unknown.

Foss, Roderick, recruited March, 1864; wounded second battle Cold Harbor; resides in Alabama.

Fortner, Richard, killed in skirmish below Richmond, January, 1865.

Floyd, Charles, wounded at Gaines' Farm, 1862; resides in Texas.

Garner, Caleb, recruited April, 1862; wounded at Gettysburg, 1863, and died from wounds.

Garner, John, recruited April, 1862; killed at Gaines' Farm, July, 1862.

Goldstein, Isadore, taken prisoner at Chickamauga; remained in prison until after the war; resides in Pennsylvania.

Gandy, Oxford, recruited November, 1861; honorably discharged July, 1862; resides in Conecuh county, Alabama.

Grice, Francis M., recruited November, 1861; lost left arm at Gaines' Farm; afterwards sutler Fourth Alabama Infantry; resides in Escambia county, Alabama.

Gaff, John, recruited November, 1861; killed at Gaines' Farm, July, 1862.

Hodo, John, recruited April, 1862; killed at Malvern Hill, 1862.

Hughes, Daniel, honorably discharged August, 1861; died during the war.

Hodges, Dr. Elias O., promoted to assistant surgeon of a Virginia regiment, 1863; died in Texas since the war.

Hodges, William, wounded at Gaines' Farm, July, 1862; taken prisoner at Lookout Mountain, 1863; died near Washington, Georgia, 1865.

Hudson, Walker A., recruited April, 1862; taken prisoner at Hagerstown, Maryland, 1863; remained in prison during the war.

Hirschfelder, Jacob, killed at Sharpsburg, Maryland, 1862.

Hyde, John D., recruited November, 1861; wounded at Gaines' Farm, 1862, and at Chickamauga, September, 1863, and in skirmish below Richmond, 1864; resides in Conecuh county, Alabama.

Hyde, Joseph, recruited November, 1861; resides in Conecuh county, Alabama.

Henderson, William, resides in Georgia.

Haskins, William, recruited April, 1862; killed at Petersburg, Virginia, 1864.

Haskins, Isaac, recruited April, 1862; resides in Texas.

Horton, William, wounded in shoulder and leg at Gaines' Farm, July, 1862; resides in Butler county, Alabama.

Johnson, William W., wounded and disabled at Gaines' Farm, 1862, and honorably discharged; resides in Conecuh county, Alabama.

Johnston, Augustus, recruited March, 1864; killed at Wilderness, May 6, 1864.

Jones, E., recruited April, 1862; honorably discharged for sickness in 1862.

Johnston, Emanuel, recruited November, 1861; killed at Malvern Hill, July, 1862.

King, J. O., recruited November, 1861; discharged in the winter of 1861; resides in Butler county, Alabama.

Kirk, Frank, recruited November, 1861; honorably discharged; joined the Thirty-eighth Alabama Regiment; killed at Chickamauga, September, 1863.

Little, J. H., resides in Texas.

Long, William B., killed at Gettysburg, July, 1863.

Lampkins, Lindsey, died at Staunton, Virginia, July, 1863.

Lynch, Fielding, recruited April, 1862; killed at Gaines' Farm, July, 1862.

Mathews, William M., died in Conecuh county, Alabama, since the war.

Mertins, Julius A., recruited April, 1862; killed at Gaines' Farm.

Mosley, Mason L., resides in Erath county, Texas.

Morris, Wiley, recruited in 1864; died in Conecuh since the war.

APPENDIX. 231

Morrow, William, wounded at the second battle Manassas, and wounded at Spottsylvania Court House, May, 1864; resides in Mobile county.

Myers, John, recruited November, 1861; wounded at Gaines' Farm, July, 1862; dropped from the roll in 1863; killed in Butler county, Alabama, since the war.

Mason, John, wounded in first battle Manassas; dropped from the roll 1862; resides in Conecuh county, Alabama.

McMillan, C. C., furloughed in 1862, and transferred to another command; resides in Butler county, Alabama.

McIver, Evander, wounded in two places first battle Manassas, and honorably discharged September, 1861; resides in Texas.

Nichols, W. H. H., deserted to enemy in front of Richmond, March, 1865.

Nichols, John, transferred from Finnegan's Florida Regiment in the fall of 1864, and deserted to enemy before Richmond, March, 1865.

Nash, Samuel D., honorably discharged August, 1861; resides in Monroe county, Alabama.

Olivia, George, recruited November, 1861; honorably discharged August, 1862; died since the war.

Peacock, Jesse, killed in first battle Manassas, July 21, 1861.

Perry, Frank, deserted November, 1863.

Perry, Owen, wounded first battle Manassas, July 21, 1861, and honorably discharged; rejoined the army, was captured, and died in prison.

Perry, Thomas, recruited May, 1864; wounded at Spotsylvania Court House, May, 1864; resides in Monroe county, Alabama.

Perry, Theophilus, recruited May, 1864; residence unknown.

Powell, Ephraim, killed second battle Cold Harbor, June 3, 1864.

Perryman, James, honorably discharged January, 1862, and died in Conecuh county, Alabama, during the war.

Quinley, William, recruited April, 1862; wounded at Gaines' Farm, July, 1862, and at Gettysburg, July 3, 1863; deserted to the enemy in 1865.

Quinley, Stephen, recruited March, 1863; wounded at Wilderness, May 6, 1864; resides in Texas.

APPENDIX.

Ray, Thomas E., recruited April, 1862; wounded at Sharpsburg, September, 1862; deserted to enemy 1864.

Russel, David, honorably discharged December, 1861, for disability; resides in Louisiana.

Rose, Robert, killed at Seven Pines, Virginia, May 31, 1862.

Robbins, John, killed first battle Manassas, July 21, 1861.

Robbins, Thomas, died from wounds received at Gaines' Farm, July, 1862.

Robertson, Thomas, killed second battle Manassas, August, 1862.

Ritchey, Thomas, recruited April, 1862; died in the hospital at Richmond, August, 1862.

Robinson, J. Mat, honorably discharged for sickness, 1862; resides in Conecuh county, Alabama.

Stearns, Henry C., wounded at Gaines' Farm, July, 1862; resides in Conecuh county, Alabama.

Stallworth, Nick, wounded at Gaines' Farm, July, 1862; honorably discharged 1862; resides in Conecuh county, Alabama.

Stallworth, W. L., honorably discharged June, 1861, for disability; resides in Conecuh county, Alabama.

Snowden, Newton, killed at Wilderness, May 6, 1862.

Snowden, William H., wounded in skirmish at Lenoir Station, Tennessee, December, 1863; honorably discharged for wounds received in 1863; resides in Conecuh county, Alabama.

Salter, Mich B., wounded at Gaines' Farm, July, 1862; wounded at Gettysburg, July 3, 1863, and right arm amputated; honorably discharged; resides in Conecuh county, Alabama.

Stallworth, Jos., killed second battle Manassas, August, 1862.

Stuckey, Buck, wounded second battle Manassas, August, 1862; killed at battle Darbytown Road, September, 1864.

Stuckey, John, wounded at ———; resides in Conecuh county, Alabama.

Stuckey, James, recruited November, 1861; resides in Monroe county, Alabama.

Strickland, James, killed first Manassas, July 21, 1861.

Smith, Jack, recruited November, 1861; honorably discharged for disability; resides in the State of Georgia.

Shaver, John D., recruited April, 1862; killed at Chickamauga, September, 1863.

APPENDIX. 233

Shaver, Phil. C., recruited April, 1862; resides in Conecuh county, Alabama.

Sheffield, Evans, wounded at Gaines' Farm, July, 1862, and at Gettysburg, July, 1873; killed by a falling tree in Conecuh county, Alabama, since the war.

Sampey, Francis M., wounded at second Manassas, August, 1862, and near Farmville, Virginia, April, 1865; died in Selma, Alabama, 1874.

Sampey, Greenberry G., recruited May 7, 1864; resides in Conecuh county, Alabama.

Thomas, James H., wounded at Seven Pines, May 31, 1862; killed second battle Manassas, August, 1862.

Thomas, James C., recruited November, 1861; killed at Sharpsburg, Maryland, September, 1862.

Thomas, Henry C., recruited September, 1862; resides in Texas.

Turk, Theodosius, wounded at first Manassas; honorably discharged under act of Congress, 1862.

Whelan, Pat S., commissary sergeant Fourth Alabama; died at Sparta since the war.

Wilson, John W., recruited November, 1861; wounded at Cold Harbor, Virginia, June 3, 1864; resides in Conecuh county, Alabama.

Wilson, George, wounded at Spotsylvania Court House, May 8, 1864; residence unknown.

Wilkinson, Thomas, deserted March, 1862.

Wimberly, Dr. Samuel H., killed at first Manassas, July 21, 1861.

Williamson, John, recruited November, 1861; honorably discharged 1862; resides in Conecuh county, Alabama.

Williamson, James, recruited November, 1861; honorably discharged 1862 for disability; resides near Brooklyn, Alabama.

Watson, Bailey, recruited November, 1861; taken prisoner 1864, and remained in prison until the end of the war; resides in Texas.

Wood, Rev. George A., recruited November, 1861; wounded at Gettysburg, July 3, 1863; resides in Georgia.

HISTORY OF CONECUH COUNTY, ALABAMA

ADAMS, JOHN QUINCY 96
   SAMUEL 206-207
ADDIEL CHURCH, 33
AKERMAN, JOHN 228
ALABAMA RIVER, 19,30,38
   51,61
ALABAMA TOWN, 80
ALABAMA, 18,73,83,168
. ALLENTON 64
. BALDWIN CO. 192
. BELLVILLE 16-17,19-20
.   24,27-29,32,40-41,43
.   48,64,83,100,105,108
.   109,116,121,124,126
.   134,136,146,158,162
.   173-174,186,201,210
.   219
. BREWTON 50,185
. BROOKLYN 34,43,45
.   47-50,55,76-78,87,101
.   125,133,159,183,186
.   204,233
. BUENA VISTA 21
. BURNT CORN 30-31,35,39
.   55,59-60,62,78,81,85
.   86,98,113,157,187
. BUTLER CO. 37,39,107
.   156,164,225,230-231
. CAHABA 113
. CASTLEBERRY 43,184-185
.   218
. CLAIBORNE 19,21,29,38
.   112,122,126,136,138
.   148

. CLARKE CO. 30,61-62,87
.   148,150
. CONECHU CO. 37
. CONECUH CO. 34,39,74
.   78,83-84,107,112,114
.   132,135,148,152,156
.   161,167,171,173,192
.   214,223,225-233
. COOSA CO. 201
. COTTEN'S BLUFF 186
. COVINGTON CO. 204
. DALLAS CO. 38,112-113
. ESCAMBIA CO. 50,214
.   229
. ESCAMBIA COUNTY 186
. EVERGREEN 20,34-35,55
.   62-63,65,87,89,106
.   117-118,148,157,171
.   173-174,177,179,183
.   192,195,198,201-202
.   205,210,212,214,219
.   224
. FORK SEPULGA 55,57,59
.   148
. FORKS SEPULGA 84
. FORT CRAWFORD 43,50-54
.   101
. GRAVELLA 158
. GREENVILLE 85
. HAMPDEN RIDGE 19-21,29
.   36,43-46,119-121,182
. HAYNEVILLE 112,132,155
. HENRY CO. 117
. HIGDON 35

HISTORY OF CONECUH COUNTY, ALABAMA

ALABAMA,(cont)
- JAYVILLA 198
- KEMPVILLE 187
- LOWNDES CO. 30,57,86
- 112,132,155,157
- MOBILE 18,30,84,100
- 134,148,155,179-180
- 202,211,214,217,225
- MOBILE CO. 107,231
- MONROE CO. 19,21,30,36
- 38-39,42,58,61,78,81
- 84,99,107,109,112,114
- 122,125-126,136,171
- 183,187,195,210,231
- 232
- MONROEVILLE 64
- MONTEVALLO 187
- MONTGOMERY 80,117,136
- 147,155,171,206,211
- 212,214
- MONTGOMERY CO. 30,57
- 228
- MOUNT MORIAH 84
- MOUNT WILLING 86
- OLD TOWN 44,55,57,62
- 91,163,201
- OLD TURNBULL 32
- PENSACOLA 76
- PHILADELPHIA 80
- PINE APPLE 116
- PINE ORCHARD 61
- PINEVILLE 58
- POLLARD 51
- PRATTVILLE 201
- PURYEARVILLE 99
- RABBVILLE 89
- SELMA 233
- SHELBY CO. 187
- SNOW HILL 134
- SPARTA 34,37,41,43-46
- 54,57-58,78,96,112
- 119,124,131,136,146
- 151,155,162,167-168
- 169,173-174,184-185
- 192,210,212,225-226
- 227,233
- ST. STEPHENS 30
- TALLADEGA 201
- TALLADEGE 13
- TURNBULL 183
- UNIVERSITY OF 13
- WASHINGTON CO. 30,226
- WILCOX 47
- WILCOX CO. 64,82-84
- 107,116,134,177,179

ALAZAN, 139
ALFORD,ARTEMUS S. 228
AMOS, 49
  MILTON 48,185-186
ANDALUSIA, 173
ANDERSON, 47
- GEORGE 228
- JOHN 162
- W.F. 227
ANDREW, 82
ANDREWS, 64
- GEORGE 63-64
- GEORGE R. 64

HISTORY OF CONECUH COUNTY, ALABAMA

ANDREWS,(cont)
. H.M. 64
. JAMES M. 227
. JAMES W. 64
. STEPHEN S. 111
ANGLE, JOHN 196
APPOMATTOX COURT HOUSE-
  E VA., 209 209
ARD'S CREEK, 47
ARKANSAS, 187
ARMSTRONG, 107
  THOMAS 102
ARTHUR, 115
ASHLEY, 87
. AMANDA THOMAS 181
. W.A. 147
. WILLIAM 195
. WILLIAM A. 127,129
. 176-177,182
. WILLIAM ADAM 180
. WILSON 55,86,101-102
. 107,110-111,137,199
AUSTILL, JERE 31
AUTREY'S CREEK, 20
AUTREY, 29,37,43
. ABSALOM 105
. ALEXANDER 19,27,36,121
. KATE 168
BAGBY,A.P. 112
  ARTHUR P. 38
BAGGETT, ABRAHAM 58
. JESSE 43
. MARTHA 83
. RICHARD 43,228

BARNETT,S.A. 202
  SAMUEL A. 134
BARNUM, 165
BASSETT'S CREEK, 61
BATTLE BRANCH, 19
BATTLE OF BOONSBORO VA-
  A., 209 209
BATTLE OF BULL RUN, 154
BATTLE OF CHERUBUSCO,
   164
BATTLE OF COLD HARBOR -
  VA., 209 209
BATTLE OF COLD HARBOR,-
  , 206 206
BATTLE OF CONTRERAS, 164
BATTLE OF FREDERICKSBU-
  URG VA., 209 209
BATTLE OF HORSE SHOE, 26
BATTLE OF LOOKOUT -
    MOUNTAIN TN. 228
BATTLE OF MALVERN HILL-
  L VA., 209 209
BATTLE OF MANASSAS VA.-
  ., 209 209
BATTLE OF SEVEN PINES -
  VA., 209 209
BATTLE OF SHARPSBURG V-
  VA., 209 209
BATTLE OF SUFFOLK VA.,-
  , 209 209
BATTLE OF WILDERNESS V-
  VA., 209 209
BAYLOR UNIVERSITY, 133
BEARD, BLAKE 228

HISTORY OF CONECUH COUNTY, ALABAMA

BEARD,(cont)
  WILLIAM 196
BECK,FRANK 177
BEE, 209
BELL, 43,105,181
 . JOHN 101,122,153
 . W.A. 111
BELLINGRATH, 217
BELLVILLE ACADEMY, 210
BELLVILLE ALABAMA, 132
BELLVILLE BAPTIST CHURC-
 . CH, 30 30,35
 . 131
BELLVILLE BRANCH, 31
BELLVILLE CHURCH, 81
BELSER,JAMES E. 136
BENTON, 105
  THOMAS H. 104
BETHLEHEM ASSOCIATION,
    35
BETTS,ED 228
 . FRANK 228
 . ISAAC 23
 . JACOB 30
 . JOSHUA 22-23,59
 . WILLIAM 60
BEULAH BAPTIST CHURCH,
    35
BIBB,WILLIAM 31,85
BIDGOOD, 150
BIG ESCAMBIAS RIVER, 95
BIG WARRIOR NATION, 27
BLACKSHEAR, 47
  WILLIAM 101

BLAKELY, 29
  G.W. 228
BOLLING,JAMES M. 111,130
    132
BONHAM, 141
BONNETT,J.B. 228
BOOKER,W.B. 228
BOTTLE CREEK, 47,215,219
BOULWARE,GIL R. 226
  MORTIMER 124,178
BOWIE, 43,97,143
BOWLES, 171
 . P.D. 209
 . PINCKNEY DOWNIE 208
BOX,BLANTON P. 106
BOYKIN, 46
  FRANK 48,76
BOYNTON,J.S. 204
BRADLEY, 174
  WILLIAM M. 166
BRAGG, 209
BRANTLEY,JOHN 47
BRECKINRIDGE,JOHN C. 153
BREWER, 50
  WILLIAM 101
BREWTON,BENJAMIN 51
BRILEY,THOMAS 227
BROUGHTON, 207
BROWN,JOEL 55-56
 . JULIUS 228
 . ROBERT 228
 . WILLIAM 228
BUCHANAN,SAMUEL 19
BUELL,DAVID 197

HISTORY OF CONECUH COUNTY, ALABAMA

BUFORD,	212	CAUSER,	43
BURGAMY, JOHN	114	CHAPMAN, HENRY C.	228
WILLIAM	114	LITTLEBERRY	107
BURK, WILLIAM	228	CHARLESTON,	153
BURNETT, JOHN D.	120	CHARLTON,	43
SAMUEL	119-120	CHATTAHOOCHEE RIVER,	19
BURNS, B.M.	195	30,38,55-56,73,105	
BURNT CORN CREEK,	16,19	CHEHAW,	211
	50,219	CHRISTIAN, ALFRED	226
BURNT CORN SPRING,	62-63	GEORGE	128,196
BURNT CORN SPRINGS,	51	CHURCH OF ENGLAND,	88
BURSON,	49	CLAIBORNE,	24
BURT, JOSEPH	25	CLARK, WILLIAM D.	227
CAHABA,	60	CLARKE, ELI	197
CALDWELL, JAMES	101	CLAY, HENRY	122
CALHOUN, JOHN C.	38	CLOUGH, JOSEPH P.	102
CALLAHAN PLACE,	45	CLUFF,	63
CALLER,	17,19	COLE, C.D.	146
JAMES	16	COLEMAN, HENRY C.	228
CALLOWAY, JOSHUA	58-59,98	WILLIAM	228
CAMERON,	47	COLLEY, BARTLEY	53
CANADA, NEW BRUNSWICK	121	CONE, JESSE	58
STANSTEAD	121	CONECUH CIRCUIT,	81
CARTER, D.L.	228	CONECUH CO. HISTORICA-	
CARY PLANTATION,	45	L SOCIETY, 223	223
CARY,	136-137,160,184	CONECUH RIVER,	26,48,51
. A.D.	110,128,135,153	. 59,76-78,80,96,186	
.	161,176	.	215
. ARMSTEAD DUDLEY	135	CONNECTICUT, BROOKLYN	47
. C.	168	. CANTON	160,162
. JOHN D.	129,147,154	. LITCHFIELD	37
. JOHN DUDLEY	165-166	CONSTANTINE, GEORGE	101
CASTILLO, P.D.	128	COOK, NATHAN	102
CATO, A.J.	229	. R.J.	51,54

HISTORY OF CONECUH COUNTY, ALABAMA

COOK, (cont)
. SAMUEL 102
COOPER, M.A. 228
CORSEY'S OLD FIELD, 106
COSEY, JAMES 63
COTTEN, JOHN A. 98
. LODDY 51
. LOFTON 51
. RADFORD 52
COTTON, JAMES 226
CRANE, WILLIAM CAREY 133
CRAVEY, 55
CROCKETT, 143
CROSBY, 41, 131
. CHESLEY 21, 40, 106-107
. HARRIET E. 178
. JOHN 106, 130, 178
. MADISON 105
. PERMELIA 201
. S. 168
. WILLIAM S. 227
CRUIKSHANK, .14
M.II 13
CUMMING'S MILL, 101
CUMMING, 23-24, 97-98
CUNNINGHAM, WILLIAM 186
 187-188
CURLEE, F.M. 228
CURNELLS, JIM 62-63
CURRY, RICHARD 47, 55
W.G. 47
CURTIS, HENRY E. 102
CUSTOM HOUSE, 49
DALE COUNTY, 82

DALE, SAM 17
DANIELS, J.W. 229
DARBY, JAMES W. 225
DARBYTOWN ROAD, 232
DAVIS, 181
D.C. 176
DEAN, DRURY 58
. GEORGE 48
. JOHN 47
. RANSOM 30
. RANSOM L. 108
. REUBEN 47-48
. THOMAS 229
DELLETT, JAMES 138
DEVEREUX, JOHN W. 102
JULIAN S. 102
DODSON, D.M. 204
DOLLYHIDE, 101
DONALD, ALEXANDER 21
HEZEKIAH 155, 158
DONALDSON ACADEMY, 200
DOUGLAS, STEPHEN A. 153
WILLIAM 229
DOWNS, GEORGE 226
JERRE 229
DUBOSE, 168
. JAMES 229
. SAMUEL 102
DUCK CREEK, 58
DUKE, WILLIAM A. 176
DUNHAM, JOHN Q. 227
DUNKLIN, J.H. 196
DYAS, THOMAS 229
E.C. SMITH MILL, 64

HISTORY OF CONECUH COUNTY, ALABAMA

EAST TENNESSEE UNIVERSITY, 181 181	. PENSACOLA 16,32,48-49
ELLIS MILLS, 24	. 51-57,62,77-78,89,117
ELLIS'S MILL, 97	. 125,147,184,208,210
ELLIS, 50,83	. TALLAHASSEE 45-46
. JOHN 98	FLOWERS,A.S. 107
. WILLIAM E. 110	FLOYD,ALFRED H. 227
ESCAMBIAS RIVER, 51	CHARLES 229
ETHERIDGE,JOHN W. 159	FOLKS, 49
ETHRIDGE,J.W. 193	FOOTE,GEORGE 64
MALACHI 49	FORBES,ABISHA 160
EVERETT, 181	. SHERMAN G. 160-162
EVERGREEN ACADEMY, 35	. SOLOMON S. 160,162-163
106,201	. SQUIRE 160
FARLEY, 58	FORT HARRISON, 229
FARNHAM,G.R. 197	FORT MIMMS, 17
. GEORGE ROBERT 210-212	FORTNER,JAMES 193,196
. JOHN H. 27,109	RICHARD 229
FEAGIN,AARON 47	FOSS,RODERICK 229
. GEORGE 47	FOWLER'S MILL, 122
. MCCONNELL 47	FRANKLIN COLLEGE, 37
FELLOWSHIP BAPTIST CHURCH, 84 84	FRANKLIN PLANTATION, 119
FERGUSON, 100	FULLER, 97-98
FERRY PASS, 53	GAFF,JOHN 229
FIELDS,JOHN 102	GAINES' FARM, 225
FINNEGAN, 231	GALLAGHER, 58
FLORIDA, 30,81-83-84,105	GANDY,OXFORD 229
. 166,168,173,231	GARNER,CALEB 229
. ESCAMBIA CO. 202	JOHN 229
. JACKSONVILLE 211	GARRETT, 182,199
. MADISON CO. 227	GATCH,LOUIS 226
. MILL VIEW 185	GAUF HOUSE, 45
. MILTON 48,163,173,186	GAUF, 45
	GENERAL PUSH, 59
	GEORGE, 81

HISTORY OF CONECUH COUNTY, ALABAMA

GEORGIA STATE COLLEGE,- , 135 135
GEORGIA, 28,30,36,45,47
   . 64,66,73,83,105,119
   . 168,209,230,233
   . ATHENS 135
   . ATLANTA 204
   . BURKE CO. 113
   . CHICKAMAUGA 226-230
   . 232
   . CLARKE CO. 37,135
   . CRAWFORD 204
   . DALTON 156
   . FAYETTE CO. 203
   . JACKSON CO. 59,114
   . JONES CO. 186
   . LEE CO. 133
   . MCDONOUGH 203
   . SPARTA 46
   . STEWART CO. 204
   . TWIGGS CO. 29,117
   . WASHINGTON 229
   . WILKINSON CO. 20,115
GETTYSBURG PENNSLYVANIA, 209 209
GODBOLD,NATHAN 106-107
GOLDSTEIN,ISADORE 229
GOLIAD, 139,141
GONZALES, 140
GOODE,GARLAND 106-108
   GILES 210
GOODLOE,BENJAMIN J. 110
GORBES,SHERMAN G. 129
GRACE,JAMES 59,101
GRAHAM, 47
   JOHN E. 102
GRANT, 163
GRAVELLA, 173
GREAT BRITAIN, 36,86
GREEN,WILLIAM 226
GREENE, 115
   . JOHN 30,59,61,99,102
   . 114
   . WILLIAM 176
GREENING,ELDRIDGE S. 47
     102
GREENSLATE, 193
GREENVILLE, 148
GRICE,FRANCIS M. 229
GUICE,JOHN G. 225
GULL'S POINT, 78
HALSTEAD, 49
HARE,JOSEPH T. 50
HARRINGTON,MILES 30
HARRIS,HARRISON 58
   S.W. 113
HART, 49
   . BENJAMIN 48,64
   . REUBEN 20
HASKINS,ISAAC 230
   WILLIAM 230
HAWTHORNE, 58,84,105
   . ALEXANDER TRAVIS 84
   . J. BOARDMAN 59,84
   . J. RICHARD 104,115-116
   . J.R. 30,109,124
   . JAMES 124
   . JOSHUA 20,31,124

HAWTHORNE, (cont)
. KEIDAR   59,79,83,98
. RICHARD   116
HAWTHORNES MILL CREEK,
                 19
HAYES,   31,60
HEMPHILL,WILLIAM 102
HENDERSON,BROCK 164
. DAVID F.   110,184
. HERNDON LEE   111
. J.M.   177
. JOHN M.   176,183,185
.   193
. L.   168
. WILLIAM   230
HENDRICKS,DAVID 101
HENRY,J.K.   152
HERBERT,JOHN   102
HERRIN,ROBERT   21
HILLIARD'S LEGION, 134
HINDMAN,THOMAS C. 207
HIRSCHFELDER,JACOB 230
HIRSHFELDER,Y.S. 147
HITCHCOCK,   107
HODGE,   49
  THOMAS   43
HODGES,ELIAS O. 229
  WILLIAM   229
HODO,JOHN   229
HOG'S CREEK,   57
HORN,DANIEL H.   154
HORSE SHOE,   26
HORTON,   49
  WILLIAM   230
HOSEFIELD,   100
HOUGHTON,   43
HOUSTON,JOHN   58
HOWARD COLLEGE, 131,199
HUDSON,WALKER A. 230
HUGHES,DANIEL   229
HUNTER'S CREEK, 174
HUNTER,   46,113
. HARRY   48,76
. J.S.   112
. JOHN S.   37,47,102
. JOHN STARKE   112
. STARKE   48,76
HYDE,JOHN D.   230
  JOSEPH   230
ILLINOIS,   153
IRELAND,   89,122
  BELFAST   88
IRVIN,PARTHENIA B. 36
JACKSON'S STORE, 58
JACKSON,   26,50-51,53,83
.   104,136,175
. ANDREW   58
. WILEY   58
JAY,   62,168
. ANDREW   61,127,138,145
.   147,198-200
. DAVID   61
JERNIGAN,   51
. BENJAMIN   50,54
. WILLIAM   51
. WILLIE   54
JOHNSON,ASA   147
. CALEB   147

HISTORY OF CONECUH COUNTY, ALABAMA

JOHNSON,(cont)
. ISAAC D. 153
. WILLIAM W. 230
JOHNSTON, 175
. ASA 47
. AUGUSTUS 230
. CALEB 47
. EMANUEL 230
JONES, 117,150,164
. A.W. 108,110-111,185
. 191,193
. CHURCHILL 106-108
. 110-111,137,158-159
. E. 230
. JAMES 48,76
. JOHN 48,76
. THOMAS P. 59
. WILLIAM 64,85,98,102
. 119
KELLY, 201
KENNEDY,A.B. 153
KENTUCKY, 153
  LOUISVILLE 113,199,201
KING HENRY OF NAVARRE,-
  , 170 170
KING,J.O. 230
. JAMES 49,79,83,98
. WILLIAM R. 126
KIRK,FRANK 230
KYSER,GEORGE 59
LAMPKINS,LINDSEY 230
LEE, 38,49,85,175
. DAVID 30,62,85,157
. GEORGE 155,157

. GEORGE L. 158
. GEORGE LASSITER 157
. HANSON 130,132,157
. ITHIEL 30
. JOEL 30,60,85-86,132
. 157
. WILLIAM 102
LESLIE,WILLIAM PERRY 129
LEWIS,DIXON H. 155
  JORDAN B. 129
LINCOLN, 118
  ABRAHAM 153,167
LITTLE BREWER CREEK, 148
LITTLE ESCAMBIAS RIVER,-
  , 95 95
LITTLE NEW YORK, 100
LITTLE,J.H. 230
LONG,WILLIAM B. 230
LONGMIRE,GARRETT 60
LONGSTREET, 209
  A.B. 135
LORD,THOMAS 56
LOUISIANA, 168,232
. NEW ORLEANS 53
. VERMILIONVILLE 37
LOUISVILLE-NASHVILLE R-
  RAILROAD, 152 152
LOWNDESBORO, 82
LUMPKIN, 135
LYNCH,FIELDING 230
MANN,W.D. 202
MANNING, 49
MARATHON, 138
MARTIN, 156-157,184,212

HISTORY OF CONECUH COUNTY, ALABAMA

MARTIN, (cont)	
. E.W.	155, 196
. EDMUND W.	155
MARYLAND,	185
. HAGERSTOWN	230
. SHARPSBURG	227, 230, 233
MASON, JOHN	231
MASONIC HALL,	45
MASSACHUSETTS,	96
MATHEWS,	168
WILLIAM M.	230
MCCASKILL, ALEXANDER	54
ALLEN	54
MCCLOUD, JOHN	46
MCCREARY,	91
. ADAM	55, 57, 90
. ELIJAH	147
. ROBERT J.	196
. WILLIE	174
MCDONALD, SARAH	89
MCGINNIS,	146
MCGOWAN, SAMUEL	208
MCINNIS, ARCHIBALD D.	225
MCINTYRE, DUNCAN	43, 109
JOHN	43
MCIVER, EVANDER	231
MCKASKILL, JOHN	179
MCKENDREE,	80
MCMILLAN, C.C.	231
MCPHERSON, MURDOCK	46
MCQUEEN,	17
PETER	16
MEEK, A.B.	17
MEEKS,	49
MENDENHALL, ELI	20
THOMAS	20, 50, 53
MERTINS, JULIUS A.	230
MEXICO,	126, 155, 163
MIDWAY,	59
MILLER,	156-157
. WILLIAM	196
. WILLIAM P.	159, 191
MINNESOTA,	
. SAUK RAPIDS	162
. ST. PAUL	162
MISSISSIPPI CIRCUIT,	81
MISSISSIPPI,	59, 82-83
	168
MISSOURI,	104
MOBILE & GIRARD RAILRO-	
OAD, 127	127
MOBILE & MONTGOMERY RAI-	
ILROAD, 65	65
MOBILE-MONTGOMERY RAIL-	
LROAD, 214	214
MOBLEY, LEVI T.	55
MOFFETT, JOSEPHINE	203
MONTEZUMA,	48
MONTGOMERY HILL,	51
MONTGOMERY-PENSACOLA R-	
RAILROAD, 152	152
MOORE, A.B.	118
MORRIS, WILEY	230
MORRISETT, JOHN	129
MORRISETTE, JOHN	111
MORROW, W.C.	177
. WILLIAM	231
. WILLIAM C.	182-183

HISTORY OF CONECUH COUNTY, ALABAMA

MOSELY,M.L.	147	OGDEN,	47
MASON L.	107	OLD BETHANY BAPTIST CHU-	
MOSLEY,ANDREW J.	226	URCH, 85	85
MASON L.	230	OLD BETHANY CHURCH,	99
MOUNT LEBANON COLLEGE,-			133
, 133	133	OLD BEULAH CHURCH,	34,36
MURDER CREEK, 20,31,36			89
. 44,54,64,97,114,117		OLD FEDERAL ROAD,	78
. 119,215,219		OLD FLAG TREE,	56
MYERS,JOHN	231	OLD FLAT CREEK BAPTIST-	
NASH,SAMUEL D.	231	T CHURCH, 183	183
NATIONAL MILITARY ACAD-		OLD SAVAGE PLACE,	20
DEMY, 155	155	OLD STAGE ROAD,	32
NETTLES,W.T.	187	OLD TOWN CREEK,	56
NEW ENGLAND,	160	OLD WOLF TRAIL,	19
NEW YORK,	88	OLIVER,	38
ALBANY	162	. SAMUEL W.	47,102
NEWTON,	219	.	111-112
NICHOLS,JOHN	231	. SAMUEL WHITE	37
W.H.H.	231	OLIVIA,GEORGE	231
NORTH CAROLINA, 20,36,49		PAGE,	152
. 66,73,82-83,159,170		. ALLEN	58,148-149
. BLADEN CO.	80	. HASKEW	58
. BRUNSWICK CO.	80	. JACOB	58
. CHATHAM CO.	41	. K.R.	150
. COLUMBUS CO.	80	. P.D.	58,151,207
. CUMBERLAND CO.	80	PAINE,ROBERT C.	28
. FAYETTEVILLE	200	PAUL,JOHN W.	112
. HANOVER CO.	80	PEACOCK,JESSE	231
. JOHNSTON CO.	85,132	PENNSLYVANIA,	
. ROBERSON CO.	80	GETTYSBURG	209,225
. ROBINSON CO.	83,200	PENNSYLVANIA,	229
. WILMINGTON	80	. GETTYSBURG 226-228,230	
ODUM,JESSE T.	21	.	232-233

PENNSYLVANIA,(cont)		. Y.M.	147
. PHILADELPHIA	38,186	. YOUNG M.	201-203
PENSACOLA BAY,	78	RANKIN HOUSE,	44-45
PENSACOLA,	217	RAY,MATTHEW	55
PERRY,FRANK	231	THOMAS E.	232
. OWEN	231	RED RIVER,	187
. THEOPHILUS	231	REDWINE,	218
. THOMAS	231	REESE,	186
PERRYMAN,	105,118	REILLY,JOHN D.	130
. J.V.	106,110,147	RICHARDSON,STEPHEN	128
. JAMES	231	STEPHEN C.	161
. JEPHTHA V.	104,111	RICHEY,JAMES	227
.	116-117	ROBERT	226
PETTIGREW,JAMES L.	135	RILEY,	58
PICKETT,	97	T.M.	58
PIGEON CREEK,	204	RITCHEY,THOMAS	232
PIGOT,THOMAS	58	ROACH,FRED G.	227
PIKE COUNTY,	82	ROBBINS,THOMAS	41,232
PIKE,ALBERT	143	ROBERTSON,JAMES	227
PINE BARREN CREEK,	38	THOMAS	232
PIPKIN,LEWIS	98	ROBINSON,	160
POLLARD,	173	. A.J.	197,203-204
POWELL,EPHRAIM	231	. C.P.	37
PRICE,	84	. EDWIN	47-48,76,186
PURYEAR,SANDY	109	. J. MAT	232
PUSHMATTAHOY,	59	. JOSEPHINE MOFFETT	203
QUINLEY,STEPHEN	231	ROEBUCK,ROLLY	53
WILLIAM	231	ROSE,ROBERT	232
RABB'S STORE,	89,101	ROUSSEAU,	211
RABB,M.S.	212	RUSSEL,DAVID	232
. POLLY H.	-	S.C.,	
. STALLWORTH	202	KERSHAW DISTRICT	112
. SARAH MCDONALD	89	SAFFOLD,REUBEN	132
. WILLIAM	55-57,89	SALTER,JAMES	102

SALTER, (cont)	
. MICH B.	232
. SAMUEL	60
. WATKINS	30
SAMPEY, FRANCIS M.	233
. GREENBERRY G.	233
. JOHN	79,88,95
SAMPIER, JOHN	88
SAN FELIPE,	139
SANTA ANNA,	139-141
SAVAGE,	43
. NANCY	210
. ROBERT	21
SC,	
EDGEFIELD DISTRICT	208
SC.,	
. ABBEVILLE COURT -	
. HOUSE	38
. ABBEVILLE DISTRICT	114
.	135
. BARNWELL DISTRICT	86
.	90
. CHESTER DISTRICT	21,40
.	130
. EDGEFIELD DISTRICT	33
.	87,89,134,138
. FAIRFIELD DISTRICT	89
. SUMTER DISTRICT	165
SCOGGIN, JOHN	55
SCOGGINS MEETING HOUSE,-	
, 56	56
SCOTLAND,	160
SCOTT,	163
JOHN	204

SCRUGGS,	48
SEGUIN, JOHN N.	143
SEPULGA CREEK,	219
SEPULGA RIVER,	26,47-48
	76
SEPULGAS RIVER,	215
SERMONS, RICHARD	57
SHAVER, JOHN D.	232
PHIL C.	233
SHAW,	52
. J.L.	20,198
. JOHN L.	200
. JONATHAN	45
. JONATHAN G.	96
. PERMELIA CROSBY	201
SHEFFIELD, EVANS	233
SHEPPARD, FRED	179
SHIP ISLAND,	174
SHOMO,	19
SIMMONS,	46
SIMPSON, RANSOM	134
. THOMAS	100
. THOMAS W.	133
SLATER, WATKINS	102
SLAUGHTER,	49
SMITH, E.C.	64
. HORATIO	107
. JACK	232
. JOHN G.	107
. JOHN W.	140
SNOWDEN, NEWTON	232
WILLIAM H.	232
SOU. BAPTIST THEOL. SE-	
MINARY, 199	199

SOUTH CAROLINA COLLEGE-		STANLEY,	122
E,	112 112	HENRY	20,116
SOUTH CAROLINA,	28,61,64	STEARN,	122
.	66,73,83,100,103,133	STEARNS,	168,209
.	135,163,168,170	. H.F.	178
. CAMDEN	112	. HENRY	168
. HOREE DISTRICT	80	. HENRY C.	232
. SUMTER DISTRICT	135	. HENRY F.	110
SOWELL'S BRIDGE,	57	. HENRY FRANKLIN	120-121
SPANISH FORT,	212	. IRENE	168
SPARTA DEPOT,	225	. JOHN S.	226
SPENCE, INGRAM	227	STEPHENS,	181
SPIRES,	45	STINSON,	
SPURLIN,	173-174	JASPER NEWTON	226
STAHL, LOUIS	227	STONE STREET AFRICAN CH-	
STALLWORTH PLANTATION,		HURCH, 84	84
	62	STONEHAM,	49
STALLWORTH,	135	GEORGE	48,76
. C.H.	107	STRANGE, WILLIAM M.	176
. FRANK M.	134	STRAUGHN, FIELDING	41
. HARRIET E. CROSBY	178	. JAMES	31,42
. JAMES A.	124,127,129	. PINKNEY	42,105
.	147,177,179-180,205	STRICKLAND, JAMES	232
.	208	STRINGER,	43
. JOSEPH	232	STROUD,	107
. MARTHA TRAVIS	134	ELY	58
. N.	197	STUCKEY, BUCK	232
. NICHOLAS	61,87,106-107	. JAMES	232
.	110,134,137,205	. JOHN	232
. NICK	134,205-207,232	SUMTER,	82
. POLLY H.	202	TALIAFERRO,	91,165
. ROBERT P.	134	CHARLES T.	226
. W.L.	232	TALLAPOOSA RIVER,	18
. WILLIAM M.	128	TATE,	219

TATE,(cont)		. JAMES H.	233
DAVID	95	. JOSEPH A.	227
TAYLOR,	102,126,136	. MABRY	21,54,107
NANCY	101	. WILLIAM	227
TENNESSEE,	18,28,73,83	THOMASON,JAMES	51
.	153,228	THOMPSON,	43,186
. BEDFORD CO.	82	BILLY	58
. KNOXVILLE	181,209	TOMBIGBEE RIVER,	16,38
.	226-227,229	TOMLINSON,JAMES	106-107
. LENOIR STATION	232	TRACIS,JOHN D.	107
. LOOKOUT MOUNTAIN	228	TRAVIS,	35,50,83,99
.	229	.	139-140,142,144,165
. MARYSVILLE	132	. ALEXADNER	98
. MEMPHIS	204	. ALEXANDER	28,33,48,96
. PULASKI CO.	182	.	106-107,133-134,137
. STRAWBERRY PLAINS	229	.	138,157
. WEATHERFORD CO.	82	. JOHN D.	128
. WILLIAMSON CO.	82	. MARK	126,138
TENSAW,	18	. MARK B.	128,154,164
TEXAS,	58,101-102,122	.	226
.	133,159,227-231,233	. MARK BUTLER	163
. AUSTIN	143	. MARTHA	134
. ERATH CO.	230	. W.B.	139
. FALLS CO.	134,226	. WILLIAM BARRETT	138
. FORT ALAMO	138-140,143	.	143
. MARLIN	227	TURK'S CAVE,	50
. SAN ANTONIO	138-139	TURK,	49
.	144	. GEORGE	125
THE BLUFF,	52-53	. LABAN	125
THE PONDS,	20,43,116,122	. THEODOSIUS	233
THERMOPYLAE,	138,143	TUSCALOOSA RIVER,	18
THOMAS,AMANDA	181	TUSKEGEE,	79
. HENRY C.	233	UNION MEDICAL COLLEGE,-	
. JAMES C.	233	, 162	162

UNIVERSITY OF ALABAMA,- 206 206,211
UNIVERSITY OF VIRGINIA-A, 208 208
VA.,
. APPOMATTOX COURT - HOUSE 38
VANBUREN, 38
　MARTIN 112
VIRGINIA, 37,66,73,158
. 164,168,206,210
. APPOMATTOX COURT - HOUSE 209
. CHARLOTTSVILLE 228
. COLD HARBOR 225,229
. 231,233
. ELTHAM'S LANDING 227
. FARMVILLE 228,233
. FREDERICKSBURG 226-227
. GAINES' FARM 225,227
. 229-233
. GLOUCESTER CO. 135
. LYNCHBURG 225
. MALVERN HILL 229-230
. MANANNAS 225
. MANASSAS 209,226-228
. 231-233
. MECKLENBURG CO. 186
. PETERSBURG 207,227-228
. 230
. RICHMOND 207,228-232
. SEVEN PINES 232-233
. SPOTSYLVANIA C.H. 226
. 227,231,233
. SPOTTSYLVANIA 209
. STAUNTON 230
. SUFFOLK 228
. WILDERNESS 226-228
. 230-232
WADDELL HIGH SCHOOL, 135
WALDROM,HARRY 60
WALKER, 60,203
. BARTLY 24-25
. F.M. 166,176,196
. FED 101
. PERCY 179
. PERRY C. 196
WALLS, 53
　THOMAS 52
WARD, 149,152
. IRVIN 148,150
. STEPHEN 148,150-151
WARREN, 114
. HINCHIE 45
. MALACHI 44-45
. RICHARD 30,44,60-61
. 112-113
WASHINGTON DC., 140,205
WASHINGTON, 115
WATKINS, 39
　JOHN 38,102,111,163
WATSON,BAILEY 233
WATTS, 176,184,211
　THOMAS 45-46,102
WEST POINT ACADEMY, 155
WETHERINGTON,WILLIAM 58
WHELAN,PAT S. 233
WILKINSON,THOMAS 233

WILLIAMSON, JAMES	233
JOHN	233
WILSON,	174
. GEORGE	233
. JOHN W.	233
WIMBERLY, SAMUEL H.	233
WITTER,	146
WOOD, DAVID	29
GEORGE A.	233
WRIGHT,	149
. JOHN	148
. WILLIAM	151
WYMAN,	14
W.S.	13
YATES, J.	193
ZUBER'S STORE,	101

www.ingramcontent.com/pod-product-compliance
Lightning Source LLC
Chambersburg PA
CBHW020646300426
44112CB00007B/257